University Academic Editions

University Academic Editions
New York - Paris - Madrid - Tokyo - Hong Kong - London

© Ricardo Roque Mateos
A Good Spanish Book! : Basic Level Spanish Course for Beginners

This publication is protected under strict international copyright laws. No reproduction of any part may take place without the written consent of the author/s. University Academic Editions. First edition 2017

A Good Spanish Book!: Basic level Spanish Course for Beginners

THE AUTHOR

Hi, I am Dr. Ricardo Roque Mateos, a university lecturer from Spain with a PhD. in Spanish Studies. My doctoral thesis specialized in a combination of teaching strategies and methods specifically designed for English speakers who learn Spanish. I have been teaching Spanish for years in different universities from several countries, as well as in high schools, and in specialization courses for other lecturers of Spanish. This book is the result of all my knowledge and experiences, so you can be sure you are in good hands learning Spanish with it.

I always had to use many different books combined and look for specific material that had enough quality for my standards, but it was hard. With this thought in mind I decided to create a book that could truly give the readers a silver bullet to master the Spanish language in an easy and effective way. As a teacher I am extremely pragmatic, as a student I always valued efficiency in the books I read, and as a writer my aim is to condense hours and hours of classes with me in a text containing all the main explanations I use, in this case, in the Spanish courses for beginners.

If you tried other books in the past, you will be very surprised to see how some things can be learned much more easily with the correct explanations. If this is your first approach to the Spanish language, you will believe it's the easiest thing on Earth, and if it's not your first try learning Spanish, you will wonder why some classical books kept complicating things when everything is much simpler than it seemed. It was not your fault as a student... it was their fault for not teaching you properly. I have seen that a hundred times.

The design of the book is part of the learning process. You may notice that the book doesn't have an index of subjects, which willforce you to take notes (I provide some space for notes at the end of the book), write on the pages, place post-its or markers, etc. to make this book something to work with and learn, rather than just something to have. The cultural information appears randomly after some subjects to allow your brain to refresh and rest a bit before the next subject. The structure of the topics is linear and designed to scroll down fast, rather than staying on a page for a long time with lots of tables and graphics. Those elements are based on some cool research articles about cognition that I don't want to bore you with... The important thing to remember is that everything in this book is the way it is for a reason, and that if you find any discrepancy or inconsistency between anything you read here and something you may have learned in your Spanish class during high school, this book is right and Mrs. Tompkins is wrong! How can I be so confident? Well I am the native university teacher with a PhD in his language who, among other things, teaches specialization courses for other university lecturers of Spanish. I am the native lecturer who teaches the native lecturers who teach non-native lecturers from your country, who teach high school teachers. I am not bragging, I am making it perfectly clear to you that you can trust this book 100% because my reputation as an academic is at stake and I must do my best.

In the next pages I will explain you some things about the Spanish language, and answer usual basic questions that can give you some extra motivation. If you feel that you are already motivated enough about learning, you can pass directly to the first lessons.
<u>Remember to have paper or a notebook with you</u> to write down words and structures you wish to remember or review later. This is important because according to several studies about neuropsychology (that you can check if that's your thing), writing down information creates new brain connections and you can remember more things. In other words, if besides reading the book you write down stuff, you will learn more and faster.

HOW TO USE THIS BOOK

You can see at first sight that this book is quite different in its organization and planning from most other books. I am perfectly aware that for people who are used to the traditional ways, the absence of an index, or a final appendix, or giving numbers to the different parts of the book will come as a surprise and cause some initial rejection. However, you should be aware that everything has been done for a reason.

An index would give extra pages to the book... it would look bigger, and that's always nice, right? For me it would be easier to conform to the traditional standards and not cause any kind of rejection. However, from a cognitive perspective, removing the index forces you to take your own notes, mark the pages you want to work with, and creates the need to familiarize yourself with the contents. There's very interesting research about the way we use books and in this case, the index has to go, so that you can make the book more practical and less decorative.

The appendix follows down the same road. Extra pages with content that has already appeared in a book. Instead of that, taking notes, writing down the interesting bits to remember, etc. will increase language terms acquisition by a minimum of 20%. When we take notes we remember a minimum of 1 of every 5 ideas, and the appendix could interfere with that process and make us lazy, thinking that if at some point we need to look something up, it will be there. This book is designed for you to **LEARN** Spanish, not as a consultation volume.

Main points to consider to maximize the learning efficiency:

-If the book is in paper format, **get post-it notes** in different colors to mark the things you need to memorize, the parts you usually come back to check every once in a while, etc. If the book is in digital format, keep notes to it, and feel free to have notes related to the pages you are interested in.

-Feel free to underline, bend the pages, **write there**... Those things we were told as kids about books being sacred won't work with language materials. This book is for you to work with, which is why the size is as it is, and the contents are presented without silly drawings or pictures of Madrid and stuff like that. Everything is practical and condensed to improve the results, so no pictures of smiling people... and I insist... take notes!

- **Check your own examples**. The practical examples and phrases that appear here are all perfectly fine, but if you try to build your own (changing words, changing plurals for singulars, etc.) you should check on internet if those things are being said, if they are being used, and if they are therefore correct. It's a good way to try the phrases we do ourselves in the absence of a teacher to correct us live.

-The book is in **a very specific order**. Don't jump subjects, don't skip them. What you can do, and will be very good is to go back to any subject as many times as necessary. Don't even doubt it... it's not a competition, so if you feel you need to re-read the damn reflexives 6 times to grasp their uses, by all means do so.

-When learning a language, don't look ahead, look back. **Don't stress** yourself thinking about the things you still have to learn. Look back and think: "Wow! Last month I couldn't even say *gracias* properly, and now I could even have short conversations in Spanish... I'm nailing it, let's keep adding more achievements to my Spanish skills step by step"

-Take your own time, but don't quit. One week you might feel like learning subject after subject, and the next week you might feel like going swimming and not touching the book even once. It's cool to disconnect sometimes to not feel overwhelmed by the things we learn, but never to the point of quitting. Even if it's just one page per month, and a quick look over your notes, a slow progress is much better than giving up on something as cool as learning a useful language.

DISCARDING WRONG IDEAS ABOUT LANGUAGE LEARNING

There are many things we have been hearing about Language Pedagogy and Language Acquisition that have been proved wrong decades ago, but are still being repeated by people who are not experts in the field, nor have learned many languages at a good level.

1. No, you cannot learn a new language "like babies do", in a natural way or whatever you wish to call it. The language structures inside our brain are already formed and established. Multiple studies have shown that an adult brain already has the methods and communication skills adapted to our primary language. Even if you could delete your native language from your brain and embark yourself in this "natural way" to learn a new one, you would need one or two adults at your service 24/7 during 4 or 5 years, pointing at things, talking to you all the time and providing you with games and materials... what we usually call: "mom and dad". It would be hard to replicate that in a classroom or with books a few hours per week. And even if you did, I wouldn't call a 6-year-old child an "expert user" of a language.

2. Forget about "Spanish time" or "Only Spanish" communication. You don't need to have two separate boxes, one for English and one for Spanish. You need to make it so that the languages you know can interact with each other perfectly and simultaneously. It's called "compound bilingualism" and it means that if you are in a room with English and Spanish speakers who don't understand each other, you are able to talk simultaneously without pauses or periods of preparation. The idea is that the same communicative skills we already have inside our brains can be expressed in different languages automatically, not translating first from our native language, not building weird sentences just because "in my language we say it like this...". This particular set of skills will make you efficient at tasks as important as translating or interpreting.

3. There are limits to proficiency in languages... Even in our own language, if we had to debate in a court of law against an experimented lawyer or in a university classroom with a Professor of Philosophy we would probably get owned very quickly. So all those stories about people who speak 12 languages are a crude exaggeration of what they understand by "speaking" them. Indeed, you can have an average level in several languages, and use grammar and structures of Latin-based languages to talk in 12 languages or more... but you can't have native-like level in 12 different things, because even natives have problems to be as eloquent as they should in specific contexts or advanced situations. If one of these guys who claims to speak 12 languages were to become a spy in WW2, he would be shot the first day... Because he wouldn't sound French, or English, or Spanish, or German... he would sound like a guy who learned 2,000 words in 12 different languages but couldn't really have a meaningful debate in most of them.

4. Current goals will change in the future. For example nowadays (unless you are reading this book in 2084... then I am talking about the past) we see a lot of girls putting hours and hours of effort into learning Korean because they happen to like the soap operas they produce and the pop songs. The sad thing is that they don't stop to think if it's the best language for them, or if a language spoken in half a peninsula is the best investment of time and effort for the future. They just saw nice TV shows and decided that South Korea was a magical land, to go down the road of learning one of the smallest Asian languages there are (compared to Chinese, for example, the numbers are scary). In a few years, in any job interview on the planet, they will be asked if they speak Spanish, French, German, Chinese or Russian... and they will realize they would have been better off learning those massive languages spoken in many countries. Of course, those girls are an extreme case of shortsightedness planning for the future, but we should be careful not to make the same mistake in our own ways... Perhaps you feel now that you don't need to learn a particular subject in Spanish, or reach a particular level, and tomorrow you realize you were wrong, so plan for the future and learn as much as possible.

5. "What we really need is some new and amazing method and technology and fireworks!" No, what we really need is to focus on the four disciplines: listening, reading, writing, speaking; and combine all the tools and technological advances we have to get better at those four things. Even if they invented language robots to have conversations with, we would just be improving our speaking skills, not really inventing something new or revolutionizing anything. Even this very same book is a mixture of strategies, grammar, vocabulary and methods that were already there. The result is better than most other books because I have tried all these things with my students for years and years of university lectures, high school classes, specialized courses, etc. but we are not inventing anything new, just maximizing the efficiency of tools that were already there. With this same logic, you can increase your skills further adapting the tools at your disposal. What if instead of post-it notes I used those electronic frameworks for pictures that change the words I see in them every 5 hours? What if I trained at the gym with flashcards of new words appearing on my phone screen as I listen to music? Any new strategy will be adding to those 4 disciplines, and in the end, it's all about understanding more, pronouncing perfectly, not misspelling too often, and being able to speak at a very good level.

Questions about the Spanish Language

1. Why learning Spanish?

You get to speak with millions of people from a minimum of 21 different countries that have it as a native language. Plus, it opens the doors to several other countries where English might not be known, but Spanish will. It has the best ratios in terms of time invested and results obtained. Increasing your business potential to 21 new markets is always better than just one or two. If you consider that people who speak Spanish as a native language are usually not very knowledgeable in English, you get a good combination for a huge untapped area of human interactions, diplomacy, investments, business, etc.

2. What if I like the language but not some of the countries that speak it?

Well, you don't need to visit them all... The best strategy is to focus on one or two countries you like and take the rest of the speakers as an added bonus. You don't need to like everyone and everything about the Hispanic culture... but crossing 21 countries out of your list would be a bit of an overreaction. At this point it matters very little whether you like it or not... Spanish is a useful resource in most English-speaking countries and you should see it as a tool to improve your communication skills, your professional success, your traveling possibilities, etc.

3. Is it difficult to learn Spanish?

Nope. In fact in all the rankings and polls it appears as one of the 10 easiest languages to learn in the world. It's not a matter of personal taste... the grammar is easy, it doesn't have declinations (meaning that the words don't change the ending depending on what they do in the phrase), and it's easy to understand due to the open vowels and clear syllables.

4. How many varieties of Spanish are there?

As a language there is only ONE. A lot of people make the wrong comparisons between Spanish and other languages. In Spanish there is a thing called the Royal Academy of the Language which has been setting the standards for Normative Spanish, as well as recognizing local words as a valuable part of the language... to be used in a local context.

There isn't a "Latin American" Spanish either... a person from Chile differs more from a Mexican speaker than from a Spanish native. It would be beautiful if all Latin America spoke the same variety, but I'm afraid in Argentina and in Peru they won't understand local terms from Cuba. So there are as many varieties and accents as regions in each country.

5. Which variety should I learn?

For a student there is only one possible option. Normative Spanish. After you know general common Spanish, you can go to live to Puerto Rico and learn cool local words and expressions, but the language, fortunately, is very well defined by the Royal Academy in terms of grammar, tenses, vocabulary, etc. so there isn't any other option if you want to speak correctly.

6. What is Normative Spanish exactly?

It's the general language, without local terms or slang that isn't seen as international or understandable everywhere. The grammar is the same all over the world, and the only thing changing is the pronunciation of a couple of letters. Since, the first Spanish grammar was written in 1492, and America started being colonized after that precise point, we take Castilian rules as the standard for the language. Anything appearing after that point is added to a language that is already established, and can't alter it unless it is universally accepted as the norm or general rule by the Royal Academy, which is formed by a group of national academies that have the mission of transmitting and sharing their views with the royal one in Spain.

7. Which accent is better?

Normative Spanish is similar between countries. The only major difference is the pronunciation of the **C** as in "thanks" or "think" in Spain, whereas in other countries it could sound like an **S**. You should learn the Normative Spanish pronunciation because it will make you avoid mixing and misspelling words, mistaking the **C** for an **S**. It's also worth mentioning that there are people pronouncing the **C** as an **S** in some regions of Spain, so it's not a matter of one country or another, it's a matter of applying the right normative sound for each letter during your learning process. Even if you establish in Venezuela and decide to pronounce that letter as they do, it wouldn't be a great deal, unless you wanted to teach Spanish... then all the letters have to be pronounced in the classical normative way.

8. How long will it take me to get a good level in Spanish?

The studies show that between 150 and 180 hours of learning and practising can get you to an upper-intermediate level (3 hours per week = 50 to 60weeks, a year or year and a half). After that the time requisites vary, but never more than doubling the initial amount to be in a fully advanced level. Those numbers are for a well-designed program with quality time. If you spend one hour learning five words and the next hour learning another five, you will understand why some universities have such poor results in their Spanish departments, while others are producing native-like speakers in 4 years. I am obsessed with efficiency and improving the results obtained by other methods, so don't jump through chapters or skip explanations. Everything is carefully planned and placed in that order for a reason.

9. Why Spanish and not some other language?

The more languages you speak, the better it will be for you. But if you look at things in a practical way, you should learn the main ones first. In my professional life I have encountered people who choose Spanish instead of English... not learning them together, or learning one and then the other... There are people in Russia or Brazil who have no idea about English but they speak Spanish perfectly. English is the main international language by number of speakers and countries where it is official, Spanish is the second one in the same terms. If instead of knowing those two you choose to go for Hungarian and Vietnamese, you will be spending the same amount of energy and time but instead of having the power to communicate with people from 50 countries, you will be able to communicate only with people from two places. That type of personal decision will weigh heavily in future job interviews, future trips, and in an overall system in which the number of Spanish speakers is growing exponentially due to academic and demographic reasons.

10. What are those graphic accents I see in some words?

In Spanish we use those signs to clarify where the stress should go sometimes, as well as to differentiate two words that are written in the same way. At the basic level you don't need to know them perfectly, just be aware that they exist, and remember to write them in the words that you recall. They are easy to understand, but we will see them in the future.

PRONUNCIATION IN SPANISH

Spanish is very easy to read, because the letters don't change much depending on the combinations that we make or their place inside a word. In English it's a nightmare for a beginner to distinguish between tough, though, thorough, through... In Spanish you have a great advantage, because if you remember these rules you will be able to read any complicated text from a very initial level and do so perfectly even if you don't understand the half of the words you are saying. It is therefore possible to address your workers, or give a public speech from an early stage.

These are the rules for reading in Spanish.

The vowels: **A, E, I, O, U,** have to be pronounced clearly and very openly. The clearer the vowels, the better your speech will be understood. There are no mixtures in vowels and we don't join them together to make sounds halfway between one vowel and another. If you see three vowels together, the three need to be pronounced clearly.

A sounds like in the English word BAR

E sounds like the English word PEN

I sounds like the English word INK

O sounds like the English word OXYGEN

U sounds like a double O in English, like in TOOTH, or like in RUTHLESS

B sounds normal (boat, bag)

C sounds normal (can, coat) but only when it goes with the letters **A, O, U**. when it goes with **E** and **i**, it sounds like an English TH (think, thought) in Normative Spanish.

In non-academic varieties from the south of Spain and South America it sounds like an S (sink, sought). When you study Spanish it's good to have the normative variety as the main one and then decide if you wish to pick up an exotic accent later on. It would be the same as learning French with an accent from Congo instead of speaking French from France. It should only be done if you plan to establish in Congo adapting to their culture, or otherwise it's better to have the normative variety with you, if not both. Another important point when doing business or communicating in general has to do with studies showing that normative or academic varieties of any language are generally perceived as more trustworthy and intelligent than exotic regional accents or dialects. If you wish to research further on the topic, I recommend you the famous study of Dr. Lance Workman from the University of South Wales about how accents that digress from the normative one are perceived less positively than the normative varieties. I would personally recommend you to pick an accent later on (if you feel it's absolutely necessary) and focus on normative Spanish during your learning process.

D sounds normal (day, dog)

F sounds normal (fast, fog)

G sounds normal (goat, grass) with **A, O, U**, and it sounds like a strong **H** with the letters **E** and the **i**. It's not an English **H**, you will have to make it much stronger, like the sound before we spit, like the International Phonetic Alphabet (IPA) sound represented by this symbol: [X]. Like a big cat hissing... Check the sound online if you must but don't end up using a normal **H**. If you see the combination **GUE** and **GUi**, it will sound as "guest" and "guilty", the U doesn't have a sound in those combinations, just like in English.

H doesn't have any sound... ever. Unless it is in combination with **C** (China, Chart), otherwise the Spanish word **hombre** sounds just like /ombre/. Why do we have a useless letter? Latin influence mixed with the evolution of romance languages, it happens the same in Italian or

French.

J sounds like that strong G from before, the cat hissing, the [X] in the IPA system, and it is so always and with all the letters. Why do we have two letters with the same sound for some vowels? The experts can't agree, but apparently the Greek origins of the letters and the Roman uses in the evolution from Latin ended up mixing. Two different ways to represent a sound that coexist. If you think about it "Jennifer" and "Gentle" are exactly the same case in English.

K sounds normal (kid, kettle)

L sounds normal (lantern, liquid)

LL is a combination that sounds like the English **J** (John, James, Jack) but a bit softer. It can never be as soft as a vowel like I, but anything between "John" and "yolk" is acceptable. In some areas of Spain it sounds softer, more like "yolk", but it's because of regional dialects and it does not constitute normative pronunciation. Pronouncing this letter like a single L is also a mistake, happening mostly to foreigners. And in former Spanish colonies.

M sounds normal (mix, mount)

N sounds normal (name, note)

Ñ / ñ is a special letter from Spanish pronounced like **NH** in other languages (España). Keep in mind that in hand writing you can write that thing on top of the **N** as a horizontal line.

P sounds normal, but with less contact of the lips (picture, Peter) instead of "point" or "party".

Q doesn't have a sound in Spanish UNTIL we add **U** so **QU** sounds like a **K** and it can only be followed by an **E** or an **i**. So the only 2 combinations for this letter are **QUE** and **QUI** and they sound like /ke/ and /ki/.

R sounds different in Spanish. Try to make the English **R** and while pronouncing that sound move the tip of the tongue to touch the front of the hard palate, and let the air flow until the tongue vibrates up and down. It's important to pronounce this letter well so train watching videos from any Spanish TV channel. This sound is the same in most varieties from former colonies so you won't have problems. This letter is strong when it goes everywhere except if it goes between vowels (a, e, i, o, u) then it will sound softer, but STILL our soft **R** is not the English one, so put the tongue in front of the hard palate and let less air pass, but don't use the same **R** as in English because it sounds strange in every single variety of Spanish. To make a strong sound between vowels we add a second **R** like in the Spanish word "arreglar" (to fix).

Keep in mind that certain consonants make the **R** more visible than others, just like in English the word "rat" differs in pronunciation from the word "oral" but it's the same letter.

S sounds normal (sun, snake)

T sounds different. Instead of touching the front of the hard palate with the tip of the tongue only, in Spanish we put more tongue surface against the palate, so the sound produced is less defined. Don't use the English **T** in Spanish because it is too strong.

V sounds totally like a **B**, I repeat, like a **B**. Those two letters in Spanish are pronounced exactly the same, and not only in the normative one, in local varieties of Spanish the pronunciation is still like a B. Basically the words "vote" and "boat" would sound the same if they belonged to the Spanish language.

W sounds normal, but it's only used for foreign words, so sometimes there are debates about taking this letter away from the Spanish alphabet.

X sounds normal (execute, experience)

Y sounds like a normal **i** if it goes alone or at the end of the word. And it sounds like the Spanish **LL** if it starts a word or it's in the middle of one. In these two last cases it cannot sound like the vowel **i** because it would be a mistake. It has the same problem as the pronunciation of LL and some regions pronounce it sometimes in the wrong way because of the mixture with regional dialects.

Z sounds like that sound we saw for **CE** and **CI**, like the English TH (thanks, think, though) but it can only go together with these letter combinations: **ZA, ZO, ZU**.

And these rules, which are not as complicated as in other languages, allow you to read correctly from the beginning of your language process. If you want to train reading, the best option is to check audiobooks in Spanish and online videos, but both from Spain and check that they use normative Spanish instead of a local accent. You can also have a look at TVE International, the official TV station from Spain for other countries; as well as videos from TVE in their national editions. If you look for documentaries from TVE2 in any video platform you can be sure the Spanish variety will be normative and as correct as possible (search: documentales TVE 2).

Remember to be careful with the H, don't pronounce it. Also, be mindful about the LL. Some people have problems understanding the sound it makes, so even in native territories you will hear some strange sounds with that letter that are not normative. The strong sounds in G and J usually have to be trained, so try to find examples of Spanish TV shows or the TVE International channel.

BASIC WORDS AND SIMPLE PHRASES

Now that you can grasp the basics about Spanish pronunciation, you can already read these useful words and sentences correctly. The stress of the voice when pronouncing words in Spanish is usually on the second syllable by the end, so for example "hola" (hello) will be pronounced as: HO – la (and remember the **H** has absolutely no sound in Spanish).

Don't be stressed if it's your first contact with the language... You don't need to understand or learn all this section today. It's just an introduction to pick up basic information and later we will see everything in depth.

Hola = Hello (as I said, the accent in the stress i son the second syllable by the end, in HO-la)
Adiós = Bye (the graphic accent over the **O** indicates that the stress is there, so adi-OS)
Gracias = Thanks
Perdón = Sorry
¿Qué tal? = How is it? / How are you? ("you" is inferred)
¿Qué tal el trabajo? = How is work? "your" is inferred)
Hasta luego = See you later (hasta means "until", so literally we are saying "until later!"
Buenos días = Good morning (**días** means days, so literally it says "good days!")
Buenas tardes = Good afternoon (**tardes** means afternoons so literally: "good afternoons")
Buenas noches = Good night (same case, **noches** means "nights")
Soy Alex = I am Alex (**soy** means "I am" for things that don't usually vary... like a name)
Me llamo Alex = I call myself Alex (A literal translation. **Llamo** = I call / **Me** = to me)
Mi nombre es Alex = My name is Alex (**Mi** casa = my house / **Mi** nombre = My name)
Encantado = Pleased (as in... "pleased to meet you")
Sí = Yes (with the accent on the **i**, it means yes, without the accent, it means "if")
No = No (we don't have "not" in Spanish, so everything is negated with **no**)
Necesito ayuda = I need help (there is no pronoun "I" as in "I need" because the ending indicates, most of the times, which person does the action.
Necesito descansar = I need to rest (**descansar** is the infinitive "to rest")
¿Puedes ayudarme? = Can you help me? (**ayudar** = to help / **me** = me , to me)
No soy de aquí = I am not from here (**aquí** = here / **soy** means "I am" for the things that don't vary).

Tengo un problema = I have a problem (**un** is the masculine article)

Quiero ver Madrid = I want to see Madrid (**ver** means "to see / to watch")

The **H** in hola should be silent. As you can see, the ending in **-S** makes plurals in Spanish, just like in English. **Sí** has a graphic accent on the vowel and that's because Spanish has that symbol to indicate a difference in stress. The graphic accent is always a diagonal line from the center towards the right: ´

Encantado ends in **-ado**, which is like the English **-ed** to form regular participles (pasts like played, cooked, charmed).

Articles / Nouns / Adjectives

Spanish has articles like in English: THE / A – SOME. The words have gender (masculine and feminine. The neutral nouns and neutral plurals are expressed in masculine, so those are easy). Usually the words ending in -O are masculine nouns, while the words ending in -A are usually feminine nouns. It's simple to remember that because most names like Maria, Tanya, Katrina, Isabela etc. are names for girls, while Roberto, Alejandro, Pablo etc. are names for guys.

El libro = The book (masculine)   **La casa** = The house (feminine)

Los libros = The books (masculine, plural)   **Las casas** = The houses (feminine, plural)

Un gato = A cat (a male cat)   **Una gata** = A cat (a female cat)

Unos gatos = Some cats (male cats)   **Unas gatas** = Some cats (female cats)

You probably remember "uno, dos, tres" (one, two, three) from the songs. Try to use the constructions we have seen so far to make these phrases (the answers after the colors):

"I have three female friends" / "I am not a cat" / "I need two books" / "I want a house"

The colors

Rojo = Red   (El libro roj**o** = The red book / La cas**a** roj**a** = The red house. **-O** changes into **-A**)

Amarillo = Yellow (L**os** libr**os** amarill**os** = The yellow houses. We add the -S for plural)

Naranja = Orange (The masculine already ends in **-A**, so it doesn't have to change. El libro naranja / La casa naranja. Only **-O** changes into **-A**, not the other way around)

Verde = Green (El libro verde / La casa verde)

Azul = Blue (Los libros verdes / Las casas verdes. We add an **-E** before the **-S**, so that it is easier to pronounce it)

Rosa = Pink (Same case as with "naranja", used for masculine and for feminine)

Gris = Grey (The plural will be "grises". Las casas grises / Los libros grises)

Marrón = Brown (Plural will be marrones)

Negro = Black (Los amigos negros / Las amigas negras. "The black friends")

Blanco = White (Los amigos blancos / Las amigas blancas. "The white friends")

"I have three female friends" = Tengo tres amigas

"I am not a cat" = No soy un gato

"I need two books" = Necesito dos libros

"I want a house" = Quiero una casa

You probably remember from the basic constructions we saw before that in Spanish we have two different verbs dividing the concept of the English verb "To Be". This is the easiest way to identify both uses.

SER = To Be, for things that DON'T CHANGE according to the speaker

ESTAR = To Be, for things that CHANGE according to the speaker + Locations

So "I am John" and "I am glad" would be two different concepts.

Soy John = This doesn't change. I am John... that's my name, just like yesterday and last week.
Estoy contento (I am glad) = This changes. I am glad now because of some good news or something like that. I wasn't glad yesterday, and I don't know if I will be glad tomorrow, but my name will presumably remain the same.

The beauty of philology is that one doesn't need to apply complicated philosophical premises when analyzing a language. It evolved through centuries, and centuries ago in the vast majority of cases if you were born in Spain you would have been Spanish by nationality. So it doesn't really matter if now nationalities change or not... philologically speaking, a nationality is something you express with **SER**, because there haven't been enough cases of individuals changing nationality every week in order to affect the language and create an exception. I understand this is an elaborate example, but it's the kind of thinking that will allow you to choose between the two verbs in new situations.

Some adjectives can be used with both verbs, and this is the case of colors. Of course, **ser** is much more common because if something is green, it will be green as a constant state. However, my bicycle can be green (its proper color) and still be very dirty after days going around the forest so:

La bicicleta **es** verde = The bicycle is green
La bicicleta **está** negra = The bicycle is black (because of the dirt. A change has occurred, and I need to clean it).

Another adjective that you can use with both verbs is "**feliz**" (happy).

Soy feliz = I am a happy person. Happiness is in me. Happiness is my usual state.
Estoy feliz = I am happy now. Something has made me happy. I was normal before and a change has increased my happiness levels. As a speaker, I reflect that change using the verb **estar**.

Professions are expressed with **ser**, because centuries and even decades ago if you were a blacksmith on Monday, you would have been a blacksmith on Tuesday or Wednesday too... However, languages evolve and there is a construction to indicate something like: "I am working in this field or position now... but this is not who I am".

Soy carpintero, pero **estoy de** camarero en un restaurante.
I am a carpenter, but I am "as a" / "working as a" waiter in a restaurant.

Finally, the exception I mentioned with the verb "estar" had to do with locations. "The teacher is in the class" and "Madrid is in Spain" are formed with the same verb: estar, even if the teacher is in the class now and ten minutes later he could be heading home; whereas Madrid is in Spain and has always been there... So this exception is actually good because it makes things much easier. It doesn't matter if the cat is on the table 20 seconds and the cathedral has been in a city for 900 years. Both locations are expressed like:

"La catedral **está** en Santiago" (Santiago is a city, not a common noun)
"El gato **está** en la mesa" (**mesa** = table / **en** = in)

Later we will conjugate both verbs, ser and estar, but for now we will check the present simple of regular verbs.

THE PRESENT SIMPLE / PRESENTE SIMPLE DE INDICATIVO

The word "indicativo" is just a grammatical term I add here in case you need to identify this tense in some other book or table for verbs. For practical terms just remember that this is the normal present (I swim, I eat, I live etc.).

In Spanish we divide the verbs in 3 groups (**conjugaciones** / conjugations) depending on the letters in which the infinitive ends (infinitive is the normal state of the verb: to swim, to eat, to live)

NAD**AR** (To Swim)

Yo nad**o**	I swim
Tú nad**as**	You swim
Él / Ella nad**a**	He / She swims
Nosotros nad**amos**	We swim
Vosotros nad**áis**	You swim
Ellos / Ellas nad**an**	They swim (ellos = masculine / ellas = feminine)

COM**ER** (To Eat)

Yo com**o**	I eat
Tú com**es**	You eat
Él / Ella com**e**	He / She eats
Nosotros com**emos**	We eat
Vosotros com**éis**	You eat
Ellos / Ellas com**en**	They eat

VIV**IR** (To Live)

Yo viv**o**	I live
Tú viv**es**	You live
Él / Ella viv**e**	He lives
Nosotros viv**imos**	We live
Vosotros viv**ís**	You live
Ellos / Ellas viv**en**	They live

As you can see, the endings -AR / -ER / -IR are highlighted because those are the 3 conjugations. For example, any verb ending in -AR will be conjugated in the same way:

Comprar (To Buy) : yo compr**o**, tú compr**as**, él compr**a**...

Hablar (To Speak) : yo habl**o**, tú habl**as**, él habl**a**...

To use these endings, you take the normal verb, remove the -AR / -ER / -IR and simply add the ending for each person. To Buy = Compr**ar** / We buy = Compr**amos**

Some verbs have irregularities in some letters in the beginning, but it's not worth it to write and memorize a list with those things because you will quickly learn to identify them and use them whenever they appear. The endings will not vary, though. And by the way... when you were reading the verb **VIVIR** you did so pronouncing both letters like a B, as you should, right?

Useful verbs and phrases (Write down the new words in the notebook)

Quer**er** (Want) Quiero comprar agua = I want to buy water

Ten**er** (Have) Tengo una casa en Madrid = I have a house in Madrid

Pod**er** (Can) No puedo hablar español = I can't speak Spanish

Necesit**ar** (Need) Necesitamos nadar tres minutos = We need to swim three minutes

Beb**er** (Drink) No bebe alcohol = He / She doesn't drink alcohol (remember the **H** is silent)

Dorm**ir** (Sleep) Duermo en mi casa si tengo tiempo = I sleep in my house if I have time

Pens**ar** (Think) No quiero pensar en mi problema = I don't want to think "in" my problem

Cre**er** (Believe) Creo que el libro es bueno = I believe the book is good

Hac**er** (Do / Make) Hago una tarta de chocolate = I make a chocolate cake

Esper**ar** (Wait) Esperan un taxi en la calle = They wait for a taxi in the street

Busc**ar** (Look for / Search) Buscamos un regalo = We look for a present

Encontr**ar** (Find) No puedo encontrar una película buena = I can't find a good movie

Lav**ar** (Wash) Laváis la ropa mucho = You (plural) wash the clothes a lot

Le**er** (Read) Leemos libros interesantes = We read interesting books

Escrib**ir** (Write) Quiero escribir un email en español = I want to write an email in Spanish

Gan**ar** (Win / Earn) Francisco gana mucho dinero = Francisco earns / wins a lot of money

Perd**er** (Lose) No puedo perder mi tiempo = I can't lose my time

Viaj**ar** (Travel) Viajáis a España cada año = You (plural) travel to Spain every year

Empez**ar** (Start / Begin) Empezamos hoy = We start today

Acab**ar** (Finish / End) Acabamos mañana = We finish tomorrow

Conduc**ir** (Drive) Conducís muy rápido = You (people) drive very fast

As I explained you before, you can see some letters changing in the beginning of some verbs in the present. **Poder** becomes **Puedo** for "I can". These changes are easy to spot and anticipate and when **Dormir** becomes **Duermo** for "I sleep" it doesn't seem strange. With a bit of practice it will be easier to remember or infer these cases, so you don't need to memorize them. Those changes usually don't apply to nosotros and vosotros so the whole irregular present looks like: P**ue**do, p**ue**des, p**ue**de, podemos, podéis, p**ue**den.

Q**ue**rer becomes Qu**ie**ro, just as P**e**rder become P**ie**rdo. That -E- in the middle tends to become an -IE- in some of the conjugations of present simple (except for **nosotros** and **vosotros**, as we have already seen). You don't need to memorize these changes... it's simpler and more efficient to let some of these grammatical features sink in, instead of seeing the language as a bunch of lists to learn by heart.

Tú / Usted -- Vosotros / Ustedes

I didn't include **usted** and **ustedes** with the regular pronouns so that we can analyze them now in detail. They roughly translate as "you sir / madam" and "you gentlemen / ladies". We conjugate them in the third person of singular and plural, so basically we conjugate them as "he / she" and "they" in order to get distance from the person we address. "Does he want chocolate?" "Yes I do, thank you". Kind of like when in Old English people said "Does My Lord require anything?" "No Sebastian, everything is fine".

The concept of distance is particularly important. Addressing somebody in Spanish by **usted** or **ustedes** has little to do with respect. People usually respect parents or friends very much and they don't address them as "Sir" or "Madam", so in some situations it will be kinder and more appropriate to use **tú** or **vosotros** than **usted** or **ustedes**. Distance in normative Spanish is basically stating that we have little to do with each other ("-Step out of the vehicle, Sir.") but that is far away from the concept of respect. Recognizing that distance is only good if there are reasons for it, so it's a way to say "I don't know you, there is distance, and I am aware of that". If we saw a woman destroying a car window with a baseball bat, using **usted** would basically signal this distance between her behavior and ours, between her and us... Criminal! We are worlds apart and... Oh! So this is your car and your dog is trapped inside? Sorry for misjudging you... Let me help you **my friend** (addressing her as tú, now).

The misunderstandings with this rule usually come from South American territories. The natives from the former colonies learned their Spanish from people who kept distance with them and even among themselves... Priests, soldiers, aristocrats, merchants etc. and they got used to a treatment that would become marginal in the rest of the world, and even in many other languages. The misunderstandings grew to the point that in some South American countries, they will address 6-year-old children as "ustedes" (you ladies and gentlemen). Luckily, the new generations in these countries are adapting to the normative uses of these two pronouns, but keep in mind that traditions might be slow to change and you can still find inappropriate uses of **usted** and **ustedes** even among family members. The best course of action is always to answer back with the same treatment we receive, so if for whatever reasons a waiter is addressing us as **usted** as part of his job, it is advisable to treat him as **usted** as well. However, every coin has two sides... if you are that waiter and a customer insists on addressing you in a friendly and nice manner and you keep putting barriers and shields, it will be just as impolite, if not more. If in doubt, keep things friendly and indicate your preference with these phrases:

Puedes tutearme = You can address me as "tú"
Tutéame, por favor = Address me as "tú", please

It is worth mentioning that even Spanish TV programs aren't a good source of real usage of these two pronouns. If you search for what goes on in the commercial breaks during a political debate, you will see the candidates addressing themselves as "tú" and switching to a formal "usted" when they are on the air, to keep the distance and the formality.

In the same line, it would be as weird nowadays to address a girl as "Miss" as it is to address her as "Señorita". Things that were considered courtesy in Victorian times are now frowned upon both in English and in Spanish, so don't let songs fool you... Addressing a young girl in a club as "Señorita" will make her and her friends laugh at how hopeless you are. Those things are left almost exclusively for very formal settings or legal documents nowadays.

When will we see the most uses of the term "usted" or the third person that goes with it? When we are customers or clients or when we deal with government institutions. For the rest of the cases, distance is not as needed as a friendly appearance.

PREGUNTAS / QUESTIONS

You will notice that questions in Spanish open with this sign ¿ And exclamations open with this one ¡ We will see some things in the future that make more sense in English than in Spanish... but this isn't one of them. Everything in English opens and closes: ( ) " " [ ] < > brackets, quotation marks, parenthesis... except for these two: ? ! And it certainly makes sense that we mark the beginning of a question or an exclamation as well as the end of it, so this is a positive point in Spanish. To write the opening question mark write a line from the top to the bottom and then a capital **C**, now add the point on the top. **Por qué** separated in two words and with a graphic accent means "why", and together in one word: **Porque**, it means "because".

¿Qué? = What?
¿Quién? = Who?
¿Cómo? = How?
¿Cuándo? = When?
¿Dónde? = Where?
¿Por qué? = Why?
¿Cuál? = Which? / Which one?

Remember that in Spanish the constructions for questions are not done changing anything or adding an auxiliary. As in many other languages, you just change the intonation and that's it. So don't try to add "do /does" and don't let it confuse you when building a sentence.
Mi casa es roja = My house is red // **¿Mi casa es roja?** = Is my house red?

¿Qué quieres comer hoy? = What do you want to eat today?
¿Quién es tu amigo? = Who is your friend?
¿Cómo viajo hasta Salamanca? = How do I travel until Salamanca?
¿Cuándo empieza la película? = When does the movie start?
¿Dónde podemos esperar? = Where can we wait?
¿Por qué no puedes dormir? = Why can't you sleep?
¿Cuál es tu color favorito? = Which is your favorite color?

¿Por qué no quiere beber? = Why doesn't he / she want to drink?
Porque tiene que conducir = Because he / she has to drive

Tener when it goes alone means **to have** (possession) if you add **que** it means **I have to...**

Tengo una casa = I have a house // **Tengo que dormir** = I have to sleep

Cover the answers with your hand and... Try to build these phrases:

1. Where can I buy water?
2. When do you want to eat?
3. Why is your friend in Valencia?
4. What can I do in the bus?
5. Why do they wait?
6. Which is your house?
7. Where can I find a shop?
8. How can I write a book?
9. When do you travel to China?
10. How does the movie finish?

Answers

1. ¿Dónde puedo comprar agua?
2. ¿Cuándo quieres comer?
3. ¿Por qué está tu amigo en Valencia?
4. ¿Qué puedo hacer en el bus?
5. ¿Por qué esperan?
6. ¿Cuál es tu casa?
7. ¿Dónde puedo encontrar una tienda?
8. ¿Cómo puedo escribir un libro?
9. ¿Cuándo viajas a China?
10. ¿Cómo acaba la película?

This, that, that other...

In Spanish there are 3 levels of pointing at things. This and that are like in English, but the third one is for things that are much far away. This pen here, that pen there, and that other pen over there across the table. As in everything else, these demonstratives (the name of this stuff) has gender and singulars / plurals so:

Masculine Singular (for example amig**o**)

Este = This...   **Ese** = That...   **Aquel** = That other...

Female Singular (for example amig**a**)

Esta = This...   **Esa** = That...   **Aquella** = That other...

Masculine Plural (for example amig**os**)

Estos = These...   **Esos** = Those...   **Aquellos** = Those other...

Feminine Plural (for example amig**as**)

Estas = These...   **Esas** = Those...   **Aquellas** = Those other...

Este lib**ro** es roj**o**, est**a** cas**a** es amarill**a**, es**os** libr**os** son verde**s**, aquell**as** play**as** son buen**as**. The last one is: "those beaches are good". Remember that we must make the endings match: plurals with plurals, masculines with masculines, feminines with feminines... **Aquellas** can also be translated simply like "those" but it will anyway give the idea that the beaches are farther away in time or space than with **esas**, like: "Oh! those beaches in the Roman Empire... so far away from us, the speakers, both in time and space... those beaches were good indeed".

Keep in mind that we will work later on with all these things that I explain you now in brief, so you don't need to understand the whole essence of demonstratives right now or I would have added 4 or 5 more pages to the subject. All in due time...

Present of SER and ESTAR

The present is a bit irregular. It still follows the basic rules we saw for the conjugation of presents, but a couple of changes appear. Pay special attention to the conjugation of **ESTAR**, since it's the one used to form other tenses. It is used as the auxiliary verb (the one that goes with the useful one in tenses like: "I am swimming").

	SER	ESTAR
Yo	soy	estoy
Tú	eres	estás
Él / Ella	es	está
Nosotros	somos	estamos
Vosotros	sois	estáis
Ellos / Ellas	son	están

If we take that conjugation of **ESTAR** and we add the ending **-ANDO** for verbs finished in **-AR** and **-IENDO** for verbs ending in **-ER** or **-IR**, we form the English Present Continuous (I am swimming, He is reading, We are eating...) We delete the endings **-AR / -ER / -IR** and then we add **-ANDO** or **-IENDO**, equivalent to the **-ING** in English (play**ing**, swimm**ing**...)

Nad**ar** = Nad**ando** / Com**er** = Com**iendo** / Viv**ir** = Viv**iendo**

Write the new words in your notebook:

Estoy bebiendo **leche** en un bar = I am drinking **milk** in a bar

Estamos conduciendo **durante** 8 **horas** = We are driving **during** 8 **hours**

Estáis haciendo **cosas interesantes** = You are doing **interesting things**

Está pensando en un **plan** para la **empresa** = He is thinking "in" a **plan** for the **company**

Están esperando un taxi **para** ir al aeropuerto = They are waiting "a" taxi "**for**" go to the airport

Estás viajando **todo** el **año** = You are travelling "**all** the **year**"

Keep in mind that in Spanish we don't wait FOR things... we simply **await** things. **Cosa** means "thing", as you probably guessed, and the adjective, like with the colors, goes after the noun. **Empresa** means literally "enterprise" but it is used more often than **compañía** which would be the exact equivalent of "company". After **para** we don't need a gerund (-ing) like in English, so we will always put a normal verb after that word: **para comer** = for "to eat" instead of "for eating". **Todo el año** ("all the year") follows the same grammatical structure as "all the summer" instead of "all year long".

CONSIDERATIONS WHEN LEARNING A LANGUAGE

Some brief comments to explain you some of the mistakes I have seen throughout the years in language learners of all kinds. Sometimes, speakers with good cognitive abilities and talent for languages perform worse than one might have anticipated if we compare them with more modest learners (such as myself in other languages like French or Russian). There are some factors we should consider to have a good strategy when learning a new language, because unfortunately energy and time are not infinite, and you don't see many experts in Linguistics speaking 127 languages... so we can conclude that at some point one is happy with the level he or she has achieved in one language, or with the number of languages they know, and the amount of energy and time we would have to invest into a new one becomes questionable.

One of the mistakes people make is to fight the language. Unfortunately languages are not exercises in perfect evolution, but rather a tool modified throughout time by speakers that will, sometimes, make no sense from a logical point of view. It's good to understand why things happen, but we will always arrive to some expression, word, or construction that will make no sense whatsoever. The frustration from such examples could affect our motivation in a negative way, and it is precisely then that we must remember a series of facts that will keep us focused and advancing at a good rhythm:

a) Languages are not an "all or nothing" kind of thing. A little knowledge is always better than no knowledge at all, so every new thing we learn makes us better and better. There is no need to hurry and no reason to get stressed about all the things we don't know. It's like a bag in which we collect candy until we say: "Yeah I have enough... I don't plan to be a lawyer in a Spanish court of justice... My level is fine as it is. I won't be entering political debates". However, anticipating your future needs in a language is risky... so my advice would be to learn as much as you can and a bit more just in case.

b) From the moment you decide to learn a language, the language becomes yours. It's a tool for communication that, especially in the case of international languages, belongs to you as much as to the people with a PhD in the area. This doesn't mean that we can change and destroy something from the inside ignoring grammar or spelling... It means that we are not outsiders to the language we are learning. We are part of it. So the question should be: How do **we** say this in Spanish? And not: How do **they** say this in Spanish?

c) Initial mistakes are cute. I can't emphasize this enough. Mistakes are part of the learning process, they are funny and they are a sign that you are learning. If you take yourself too seriously and, become self-conscious or even offended when someone corrects you, you will not be doing yourself any favors. Laughing at mistakes is a good way to deal with them. It gives a clear notice that what you said was wrong, and it also makes you remember them for the future. Ignoring mistakes, avoiding the corrections or thinking that it's all nice and good as long as people understand what you say is short-term denial and long-term frustration. If you stop caring about your mistakes, you stop correcting them, and you stop advancing altogether. So, always further, always better, until you are the one who has to explain natives one or two things about their language.

d) Vocabulary can't be acquired without context. Some sort of context... Any context. You can't just go to the dictionary, look for a word in your language and translate it just like that. Is this word used in Spanish? Will it sound strange? Has it fallen out of use since the decades in which the dictionaries that were re-edited to create this other dictionary were published? Lexicography (the writing dictionaries thing...) can't revise all the words of a whole language for each new edition of a volume, so sometimes we find words that were already old-fashioned when the original edition of a dictionary was published, and 12 editions later it's still there... "-How do you do my kind sir? Basking in the ambience of this fine morning stroll?" "-Dude... what? Not even my grandpa speaks like that anymore".

e) Local terms and expressions have to be acquired carefully. People have a conscious or unconscious desire to propagate and expand their own views of the world, so before acquiring a new term we need to confirm it a minimum of 3 times, with 3 different sources. I remember a show that kept using the word "vicariously" in English, I adopted it to my explanations and classes, but I had to stop and explain every time what the term meant... to people who had English as their first language. So I had obviously acquired a cool word, but had to understand the settings and limitations in its use instead of just throw it around too often. The same thing happens with local slang. The coolest thug in Australia will sound like a weirdo if he uses his slang in New York.

f) Languages are not a commitment... If you have an objective to achieve (a job offer, an impending trip, an exchange program, etc.) then you must plan your efforts according to your time and energy. Otherwise, if you are just learning at your own speed, you can work on your Spanish today 30 minutes, in three weeks 7 minutes, two months later 8 hours straight of writing, reading, movies... If you organize yourself without feeling guilty, Spanish becomes a hobby to fill a lunch break. That's perfectly fine. At the end of the year you keep adding and adding more material and information to your overall knowledge. Learning a language as a hobby is also possible and although it might take a bit longer, you will notice less stress if any at all.

A Past and a Future formed with presents: Pasado Inmediato / Futuro Inmediato

Do you remember the verb **acabar** from before? With that present and this construction you get the English equivalent of: "I have just seen", "he has just eaten", "we have just cooked".

Acabo, acabas, acaba, acabamos, acabáis, acaban + DE + INFINITIVE (the normal verb)

Acabo de ver = I have just seen
Acaba de comer = He has just eaten
Acabamos de cocinar = We have just cooked
Acaban de encontrar un taxi = They have just found a taxi

Easy, right? The translation has to be like that. It's not simply a Present Perfect... the particle "just" changes the whole meaning in English, and it's only through that particle that we reach this meaning in Spanish so: **Acabo de visitar España** = I have just visited Spain. Not 3 years ago... the "just" makes it immediate and close to us in time.

In the same way, we can also make the Present Continuous from English in a very simple way and with a present. This is the present of the verb IR (to go):

yo voy, tú vas, él /ella va, nosotros vamos, vosotros vais, ellos van (I go, you go, he goes...)

As you can see, the endings of this "irregular" verb are the same as in the verb **ESTAR**, so even in irregular verbs we can find similar patterns. Mixing this present with verbs in infinitive and the word **A** (to) we get the Present Continuous:

Voy **a** comprar = I am going to buy

Van **a** dormir = They are going to sleep

Vas **a** conducir tres horas = You are going to drive 3 hours

Vais **a** necesitar agua = You (you people) are going to need water

Remember to add the **A** in the middle so that the formula is complete.

Adding vocabulary

Keep in mind that you already know some Spanish words. Here are some international words that we can also use in Spanish: Bar, Sandwich, Taxi, Parking, Manager, Marketing, Pub, Television, Radio, Cafetería /Café, Gas, Ticket.

The names of minerals and elements in Latin, sciences and medical specialties are also quite similar: Carbono, Sulfuro, Cardiología, Urología etc. Only the endings change a bit.

The words of Latin origin are changed very easily from English:
Action = Acción, Extraction = Extracción, Constelation = Constelación etc.

Latin and Greek adverbs such as: Rarely, Purely, Naturally etc. change with the endings:
-amente or **-mente**: Rarely= Raramente, Purely= Puramente, Naturally= Naturalmente.
Purely Latin expressions don´t change: Gratis, Pro forma, Quid pro quo.
Word finishing in the Greek suffix **-ist** in English come to Spanish as **-ista** except for some exceptions like "scientist" (científico): analyst= analista.

The Latin and Greek prefixes and suffixes also exist in Spanish:

Re = Again / Revision= Revisión

Anti = Against / Anti-terrorist = Antiterrorista
Trans = Through / Transport = Transporte

English words ending in **-ENT** or **-ANT** when they have a classical origin they come to Spanish ending in **-TE**: President = Presidente, Important = Importante. Words like: Impact, Tact, Contact etc. will be in Spanish like: Impacto, Tacto, Contacto.

In some words you will see sufixes (endings that make the word smaller or bigger, or funny, like in Bill = Billy) some of the most common ones in Spanish are these:
-ito / -ita = Makes thing smaller (casa = house / casita = little house)
-illo / -illa = Makes things smaller and less formal (chico = a boy / chiquillo = a little boy)
-ete = Makes things funny (sol = sun / solete = sunnily didly or something like that)
-ote = Makes things big and less formal (Macho = male / Machote = Super male!)
-ón = Makes nouns big (un problema = a problem / un problemón = a huge problem)
-azo = makes nouns and actions big (ladrillo = brick / ladrillazo = a huge hit with a brick)

These are not examples to memorize, it's just an introduction to those endings that sometimes we will see at the end of some words, to understand why they are there.

Vocabulary about TIME

Lunes = Monday, **Martes** = Tuesday, **Miércoles** = Wednesday, **Jueves** = Thursday, **Viernes** = Friday, **Sábado** = Saturday, **Domingo** = Sunday

Primavera = Spring, **Verano** = Summer, **Otoño** = Autumn, **Invierno** = Winter

Enero = January, **Febrero** = February, **Marzo** = March, **Abril** = April, **Junio** = June, **Julio** = July, **Agosto** = August, **Septiembre** = September, **Octubre** = October, **Noviembre** = November, **Diciembre** = December

Useful Words

Bus = Bus	**Barco** = Ship	**Avión** = Plane	**Coche** = Car
Hombre = Man	**Mujer** = Woman	**Chico** = Boy	**Chica** = Girl
Niño = Little boy	**Niña** = Little girl	**Jefe** = Boss	**Policía** = Police

Padre = Father	**Madre** = Mother	**Hijo** = Son	**Hija** = Daughter
Hermano = Brother	**Hermana** = Sister	**Primo** = Cousin	**Prima** = Cousin (fem.)
Abuelo = Grandpa	**Nieto** = Grandson	**Abuela** = Grandma	**Nieta** = Grandaughter
Tío = Uncle	**Tía** = Aunt	**Papá** = Dad	**Mamá** = Mom
Playa = Beach	**Empresa** = Company	**Oficina** = Office	**Fiesta** = Party

Mi padre es policía = My father is a policeman (in general, without the article **un**)

Tengo un hermano en Australia = I have a brother in Australia

El coche de mi abuelo es gris = The car of my grandfather is grey

Los trenes en España son amarillos = The trains in Spain are yellow

Tengo un barco verde, mi jefe tiene uno rojo = I have a green ship, my boss has a red one

El hijo de mi amiga está en Madrid = The son of my friend is in Madrid

¿Dónde puedo encontrar la oficina de tu madre? = Where can I find your mother's office?

¿No necesitas ayuda para ir a la playa? = Don't you need help to go to the beach?

Mi primo acaba de comprar un barco rojo = My cousin has just bought a red ship

Una amiga de mi tio va a viajar en avión = A friend of my uncle is going to travel by plane

Notice how in the last phrase we see that in Spanish you don't travel "by plane" you travel "in a plane", so always use the preposition **en** = **in** when talking about transports.

The Numbers

1 UNO	2 DOS	**3 TRES**	4 CUATRO	**5 CINCO**	6 SEIS
7 SIETE	8 OCHO	**9 NUEVE**	10 DIEZ	**11 ONCE**	12 DOCE
13 TRECE	14 CATORCE	**15 QUINCE**	16 DIECISEIS	**17 DIECISIETE**	
18 DIECIOCHO	**19 DIECINUEVE**	20 VEINTE	**21 VEINTIUNO**	22 VEINTIDÓS	

After **veinte**, all the numbers will be made adding 1,2,3 etc. (veintiuno, veintidós, veintitrés etc.) and in one word.

30 TREINTA   40 CUARENTA   **50 CINCUENTA**   60 SESENTA   **70 SETENTA**

80 OCHENTA   **90 NOVENTA**

After the number **30** they are written in 3 words, but formed exactly in the same way:

VEINTICUATRO (24)   VEINTICINCO (25)   **TREINTA Y UNO (31)**   TREINTA Y SIETE (37)

CUARENTA Y OCHO (48)   CINCUENTA Y NUEVE (59)   **NOVENTA Y TRES (93)**

The hundreds also follow a pattern so they will be easy to form:

100 CIEN (when the number goes alone)   **100 CIENTO...** (when another number follows after)
101 CIENTO UNO   **104 CIENTO CUATRO**   113 CIENTO TRECE
146 CIENTO CUARENTA Y SEIS   175 CIENTO SETENTA Y CINCO   **100 CIEN**
139 CIENTO TREINTA Y NUEVE   **198 CIENTO NOVENTA Y OCHO**   200 DOSCIENTOS
300 TRESCIENTOS   400 CUATROCIENTOS   **500 QUINIENTOS**   600 SEISCIENTOS
700 SETECIENTOS   800 OCHOCIENTOS   **900 NOVECIENTOS**

As you can see, the numbers **500, 700** and **900** are irregular, since they have some change or missing letter from the regular pattern. The thousands are formed as follows:

1.000 MIL   2.000 DOS MIL   **3.000 TRES MIL**   4.000 CUATRO MIL etc.

The thousands are totally regular, but remember that they don´t have plural, we just add the word **mil** after them and that's it.

1.000.000 UN MILLÓN   2.000.000 DOS MILLONES   3.000.000 TRES MILLONES etc.

Examples /Ejemplos

45,007   Cuarenta y cinco mil siete

322,515   Trescientos veintidós mil quinientos quince

2,809,371   Dos millones ochocientos nueve mil trescientos setenta y uno

The Spanish **billón** is the equivalent to one million of millions, keep it in mind whenever you translate an amount from English.

Sumar = To add / **Restar** = To substract / **Multiplicar** = To Multiply / **Dividir** = To Divide

Now that we know the numbers, it will be possible to say the time in Spanish. The questions are like this:

¿**Qué hora es?** = What time is it? (literally: "what time is?")
Qué hora tienes? = What time "do you have"?
¿**Qué hora tiene?** = What time "do you have, Sir / Madam"?

The response to these questions is singular if the time is 1:00 or 13:00 and whatever minutes are there. And it will be plural for the rest of the hours.

1:36 = Es la una y treinta y seis
2:48 = Son las dos y cuarenta y ocho
18:20 = Son las seis y veinte
13:10 = Es la una y diez
19:12 = Son las siete y doce

Just like in English, the quarters and the halves have their own names. Quarter = **cuarto** / Half = **media**. And just like in English, when we pass the minute 30, sometimes we express the time as "TO", which in Spanish will have the equivalent of "**menos**". The "o'clock" thing in Spanish is said like: "**en punto**" (on point).

10:15 = Son las diez y cuarto
11:30 = Son las once y media
12:45 = Es la una menos cuarto (a quarter to one / "it's one minus a quarter")
14:50 = Son las tres menos diez (It's 10 minutes to three)
16:00 = Son las cuatro / Son las cuatro en punto (It's four / four o'clock)

The dates in Spanish (and everywhere in the world except for a couple of places) are said in order, from the smallest to the biggest. **Day / Month / Year**.

4 / 12 / 2036 = cuatro de diciembre del dos mil treinta y seis
18 / 01 / 2022 = dieciocho de enero del dos mil veintidós

Strange as it is, the idiomatic habit among speakers is that the years before 2000 have only DE (Enero de 1935) whereas the years that come afterwards have DEL (enero del 2082). It's not a rule written in stone, but it's worth remembering those habits. Keep in mind that in Spanish we **don't cut the years in half**, so 2030 will never be "twenty thirty", but "dos mil treinta" (two thousand thirty). A very important rule lots of native speakers usually forget is that the years **DO NOT HAVE A DOT** for the thousands, just like in English. 2062 = correct / 2.062 = wrong

The ordinals (first, second, third...)

In Spanish there are ordinals for most numbers, but fortunately the use is limited to 10 in everyday cases, and after that number, even though the complex ordinal forms exist, we switch to the common cardinal numbers (eleven, twelve, thirteen...).

Primero (1st), **segundo** (2nd), **tercero** (3rd), **cuarto** (4th), **quinto** (5th), **sexto** (6th), **séptimo** (7th), **octavo** (8th), **noveno** (9th), **décimo** (10th).

After those, we do have ordinals like **quincuagésimo séptimo** (57th) but nobody will be using them because they are extremely limited to official or academic environments, so instead we will hear: "La cincuenta y siete edición de los Oscars" = The 57 edition of the Oscars.

As an interesting fact, it's worth mentioning that 11th and 12th have two ways to be said.
11th = undécimo / décimo primero
12th = duodécimo / décimo segundo
13th = décimo tercero

Since the rest of the numbers follow the **décimo + something** style, I would recommend you to use those whenever they are needed. However, inside an elevator, after the 10th floor, we will talk about "el piso once, el piso doce..." = the 11th floor, the 12th floor... (**piso** = floor talking about stories inside a building or flats / apartments, floor as in "ground" is **suelo**)

Keep in mind that **primero** and **tercero** will lose the final **-O** if an element follows:

-Mi amigo es el **primero** en llegar = My friend is the first one to arrive ("in arriving")
-El **primer** libro de la tienda = The first book in the store

Basic Adjectives

Contento = Happy (Glad)　　　　　　Triste = Sad

Fuerte = Strong　　　　　　　　　　Débil = Weak

Alto = High/Tall (people and things)　Bajo = Short/Low

Grande = Big　　　　　　　　　　　Pequeño = Small/Little

Rápido = Fast　　　　　　　　　　　Lento = Slow

Interesante = Interesting　　　　　　Aburrido = Boring

Guapo = Handsome/Pretty (people)　Feo = Ugly (things/people)

Bonito = Pretty/Beautiful (things)

Agradable = Nice　　　　　　　　　Desagradable = Unpleasant

Simpático = Nice/Funny　　　　　　Antipático = Rude

Gordo = Fat　　　　　　　　　　　Delgado = Thin/Slim

Rico = Rich　　　　　　　　　　　　Pobre = Poor

Enfermo = Ill/Sick　　　　　　　　　Sano = Healthy

Caro = Expensive　　　　　　　　　Barato = Cheap

Ligero = Light　　　　　　　　　　　Pesado = Heavy

Fácil = Easy　　　　　　　　　　　Difícil = Difficult

Sencillo = Easy　　　　　　　　　　Complicado = Complicated

Lleno = Full　　　　　　　　　　　Vacío = Empty

Largo = Long　　　　　　　　　　　Corto = Short

Listo = Clever　　　　　　　　　　Tonto = Fool/Silly

Inteligente = Intelligent

Claro = Clear/Light　　　　　　　　Oscuro = Dark

Nuevo = New　　　　　　　　　　　Viejo = Old (people / things)

Joven = Young　　　　　　　　　　Mayor = Old (people)

　　　　　　　　　　　　　　　　　Antiguo = Old / Antique (things and people)

We have seen already how the adjectives go after the name:

casa roja = right / roja casa = wrong. This will always be so, except with these two exceptions:

-In poetry the adjectives are sometimes used the other way around as a literary resource.

-With some adjectives like Bueno = Good / Malo = Bad. It is common to see them change position depending on the meaning we want to convey. If we put them at the beginning of a word, the final **-O disappears**. Originally the meanings would be:

Un buen perro = A good dog, a dog that is efficient at barking, hunting, protecting etc.

Un perro bueno = A good dog, a dog that behaves in a caring way and doesn't bite its owner.

However, nowadays after decades of use and evolution, even in normative Spanish it is hard to perceive the difference in some cases like: "buen hombre / hombre bueno" where both could indicate there is an absence of evil in a man. Luckily, these uses are too advanced for now so you shouldn't worry about them at this point. It would be like trying to understand the question: "Do you work hardly or you hardly work?" for an initial student of English.

Notice that the adjective **viejo** can be used for people, but it would sound a bit harsh, so it's a bit more polite to describe an old person as **mayor**. The adjective **antiguo** applied for people would mean "old-fashioned" whereas for things it's just "antique", old with some history to it.

FUTURE TENSE / FUTURO SIMPLE

Now we will learn how to form the Simple Future (I will eat, he will swim, they will sleep) in Spanish. The classical approach is to say that there are 3 endings in future, but with a simple trick we can simplify this to only one ending valid for all the verbs in future.

The trick is to remove the **-R** from the infinitive (the verb in its original form) and then, start adding these endings:

-re / -ras / -rá / -remos / -réis / -rán

If we choose a random verb, and we take away the final **-R**, and then we add these endings, a verb like COMER in future becomes:

Comer (minus the final **R** = **Come-** plus the endings **-re, -ras, -rá**...)

I will eat =	Comer**é**
You will eat =	Comer**ás**
He / She will eat =	Comer**á**
We will eat =	Comer**emos**
You will eat =	Comer**éis**
They will eat =	Comer**án**

Keep in mind that short verbs follow the same pattern, no matter how short they may be:

IR = to go, in future, after removing the -R and adding the endings= iré, irás, irá, iremos... (I will go, you will go, he / she will go...)

Tomorrow we will go to a party = Mañana iremos a una fiesta.

On Monday they will buy a house in Corunna = El lunes comprarán una casa en La Coruña.

In autumn, my brother will be in Salamanca = En otoño, mi hermano estará en Salamanca.

On Sunday I will visit your office = El domingo visitaré tu oficina.

Will you eat with us in March? = ¿Comeras con nosotros en Marzo?

They will travel a lot this year! = Viajarán mucho este año

CONDITIONAL TENSE / CONDICIONAL SIMPLE

The conditional is the tense that has "**would**" in English, followed by the verb. We will use the same trick of removing the final -R of the verb in infinitive and then adding these endings:

-ría / -rías / -ría / -ríamos / -ríais / -rían

As with the previous tense, we must take a normal verb, remove the -R at the end and place these endings, in the same way we did before:

Hablar (minus the final R = Habla- plus the endings-**ría**, **-rías**, **-ría**...)

I would speak =	Habla**ría**
You would speak =	Habla**rías**
He / She would speak =	Habla**ría**
We would speak =	Habla**ríamos**
You would speak =	Habla**ríais**
They would speak =	Habla**rían**

I would play football, but I don't have time now = Jugaría al fútbol, pero no tengo tiempo ahora.

They would buy a car, but they don't have money = Comprarían un coche pero no tienen dinero.

If I am in China, I would speak Chinese = Si estoy en China, hablaría chino.

I would like to watch a movie = Me gustaría ver una película

Dormiría más tiempo, pero tiene que trabajar = He/She would sleep more time, but he/she has to work.

Remember that the first and third person coincide (yo dormiría / el - ella dormiría) so if the pronoun is not mentioned, you need to use the context to find out who the subject is. In cases where there can be doubts about the subject, it is totally fine to use the pronouns. They are not totally banished from the language and they can be useful in times like these.

There are a couple of irregularities with the future and the conditional. They can be grouped and summarized in one simple rule. "If there is an extra **i** or **e** that makes the pronunciation slower, they will be omitted or substituted by a **d** in the verbs where they appear"

Salir (instead of "saliré" the **i** is substituted by a **d**) = Sal**d**ré, sal**d**rás / Sal**d**ría, sal**d**rías...
Venir (instead of "veniré" the **i** is substituted by a **d**) = Ven**d**ré, ven**d**rás... / Ven**d**ría...
Tener (instead of "teneré" the **e** is substituted by a **d**) = Ten**d**ré, ten**d**rás / Ten**d**ría, ten**d**rías...
Saber (instead of "saberé" the **e** is omitted) = Sa**b**ré, sa**b**rás / Sa**b**ría, sa**b**rías...
Poder (instead of "poderé" the **e** is substituted by a **d**) = Po**d**ré, po**d**rás / Po**d**ría, po**d**rías...

After some practice it will be easy to identify which verbs require these changes. There are only a few and those five are the most used, so if you remember the endings and this last rule, the future and the conditional are simple as that.

PRETÉRITO PERFECTO COMPUESTO / PRESENT PERFECT

It's also a very simple construction that is the equivalent of the English: **I have + participle**
It's formed in Spanish with the verb "to have" = **haber,** in present (just like in English) and then adding the participle of the next verb.

To form a participle in Spanish, we do the following: If the verb in infinitive ends in **-AR**, we take away those two letters and add the ending **-ADO**.
Example: Nad**ar** (to swim) = Nad**ado** (swam... "swimmed" if it were regular, which it isn't).

If the verb in infinitive ends in **-ER / -IR**, we take away those two letters and, just like before, add the ending **-IDO**.
Example: Com**er** (to eat) = Com**ido** (eaten) / Viv**ir** (to live) = Viv**ido** (lived)

The present of the verb HABER (to have) is as follows:
Yo **he** / Tú **has** / Él - Ella **ha** / Nosotros **hemos** / Vosotros **habéis** / Ellos **han**

After adding the participle we want, the examples would be like this:

Yo **he vivido** en España = I have lived in Spain

Nosotros **hemos comprado** una casa = We have bought a house

Tú **has sabido** la respuesta = You have known the answer (respuesta = answer)

Ellos **han visitado** Cantabria = They have visited Cantabria

Ella **ha estado contenta** todo el día = She has been happy all day (todo el día = all day long)

Vosotras **habéis tenido** tiempo = You (feminine, you girls) have had time

Remember that I am writing the pronouns (yo, tú, nosotros...) just so that you can identify the constructions now that you are seeing them, but as a general rule, in Spanish we don't mention these pronouns all the time because each person has a different ending, so in conversation or writing, when there's no possibility of mixing anything up, we say: "**he comido** mucho" (I have eaten a lot) and we don't mention "yo" anywhere.

Keep in mind that some participles are irregular and they can't be formed simply adding **-ADO** or **-IDO** at the end. The source of this irregularities is in most cases the Latin language, from which Spanish evolved after centuries. The irregular participles are just a few and similar verbs can be formed in the same way, unlike irregular participles in English, so it's not that difficult.

From the verbs we have seen so far, we encounter 3 irregulars:

Hacer (to do / to make) is not formed in participle as "hacido", the participle is **HECHO**

Escribir (to write) is not formed in participle as "escribido", the participle is **ESCRITO**

Ver (to see) is not formed in participle as "veido", the participle is **VISTO**

We will see some other irregular participles in the future, but they will be fewer than in English. As a general rule: he cocinado, has cocinado, ha cocinado, hemos cocinado, etc. (I have cooked, you have cooked, he/she has cooked, we have cooked, etc.)

Prepositions and Adverbs

As with the rest of the vocabulary, it's good to learn it inside phrases and with the correct context, but it can also be useful to have everything together in case you wish to review the words by subject, or you need to refresh some of them. These basic adverbs and prepositions are much needed because of their frequency and common use in Spanish.

Place / Lugar

Aquí = Here / **Acá** = Here (second version) / **Allí** = There / **Allá** = There (second version) / **Lejos** = Far / **Cerca** = Near, Close / **Fuera** = Outside / **Dentro** = Inside / **Encima** = Over, On top / **Debajo** = Under, Below / **Delante** = On the front / **Detrás** = Behind / **Enfrente** =

Opposite to (in front of something) / **Al lado** = Next to (beside) / **Alrededor** = Around

Time / Tiempo

Ahora = Now / **Después** = Later / **Ayer** = Yesterday / **Hoy** = Today / **Mañana** = Tomorrow / **Pasado mañana** = The day after tomorrow / **Anteayer** = The day before yesterday / **Luego** = Later / **Tarde** = Late / **Pronto** = Soon / **Temprano** = Early / **Entonces** = Then / **Siempre** = Always / **Nunca** = Never / **Jamás** = Never ever / **A veces** = Sometimes / **Mientras** = While **Durante** = During

Amount / Cantidad

Mucho = A lot (much) / **Poco** = A bit (little of something) / **Todo** = Everything / **Bastante** = Enough / **Algo** = Something / **Alguien** = Someone / **Algún** = Some (one element, singular) / **Nada** = Nothing / **Nadie** = Nobody / **Ningún** = no + element (Example: no animal is here = ningún animal está aquí) / **Demasiado** = Too much / **Tanto** = So much / **Apenas** = Barely / **Más** = More / **Menos** = Less

Affirmative- Negative / Afirmación - Negación

También = Too (also) / **Tal vez** = Maybe / **Quizás** = Perhaps / **Ni siquiera** = Not even / **Aún** = yet / **Todavía** = Still

Adverbs ending in -ly / Adverbios acabados en -amente / -mente

Rápido = Quick (adjective) / **Rápidamente** = Quickly (adverb formed adding -ly)
Lento = Slow (adjective) / **Lentamente** = Slowly (adverb formed in -ly)

Latin expressions / Expresiones latinas

Bis = twice / **Circa** = close to / **Gratis** = free / **Ergo** = therefore / **Idem** = in the same way

Useful prepositions / Preposiciones útiles

a = to / **ante** = before (in the presence of something) / **bajo** = under something / **con** = with / **contra** = against / **de** = of / **desde** = from / **en** = in / **entre** = between, amid / **hacia** =

towards / **hasta** = until / **para** = for / **por** = by / **según** = according to / **sin** = without / **sobre** = about something / **tras** = after something (figurative speech)

The forms **aquí** and **allí** show more prevalence in Spain and in a few more countries, whereas the forms **acá** and **allá** show more prevalence in Latin America, although it is good to remember that the four forms are used and recognized in all the countries.

The adverbs appear alone if they end a sentence, but if they are in the middle they might need connectors, just like in English: I am close = **Estoy cerca** / I am close to him = **Estoy cerca <u>de</u> él**. The particle **de** is the most used one, and it literally translates as "of", therefore in Spanish the last sentence would be understood as: "I am close of you". Después = after / Después de ti = after "of" you. As you can see, in English there's no consistency about when to use connectors with adverbs (close to you / near you, not near to you). In Spanish the Latin grammar had a bigger influence and therefore most adverbs and constructions will follow these rules: Fuera **de** la casa = outside the house, Dentro **de** la casa = inside the house, Lejos **de** la casa = far from the house, etc.

Jamás is a stronger negation than a simple "never", some sort of "whatsoever" but applied to an adverb of time. No he visitado China **jamás** = I have never ever visited China (not even for 5 minutes, I haven't set foot there whatsoever).

Apenas = barely, is used as in English, but if that's not your native language, remember that it means something like "at a minimum level".
¿Hablas español perfectamente? = Do you speak Spanish perfectly?
No, **apenas** acabo de empezar a aprender = No, I have barely started to learn

Quizás = perhaps is also written without the final **-S**. Both ways are correct and not bound to geographical habits, but to personal ones. The same person might use both in cases where adding an **-S** separates the word from another one starting with an **A**. (Quizás antes...)

Latin adverbs are a bit more usual in Spanish, but as in many other languages, they can be considered too formal or academic and they are not thrown into casual conversation, or they would seem to be out of place.

The difference between **PARA** and **POR** is difficult if you just translate all the cases from English, but if you translate them and think if the action has an origin or a destination, then you will be right more times, since Spanish is less flexible when applying one or the other.

Por = By (origin)

Para = For (destination of the action)

"We drive **by** this road **for** going to Madrid" = Conducimos **por** esta carretera **para** ir a Madrid. Notice that in sentences like these in English we use -**ING** only because the word for appears, so since that rule is not present in Spanish, we use the indicative **IR** (to go) instead of "**going**" The origin of the action or means to perform it is the road, so it goes with **por** (by), our destination is Madrid so it goes with **para** (for).

In some cases, the English translation doesn't match, which is precisely when we need to think about origins and destinations to use the proper preposition in Spanish:

This email is for me = Este email es **para** mí. (I am the destination of this email, the recipient)

This email is for (because of) my birthday = Este email es **por** mi cumpleaños.

(cumpleaños = birthday, literally "fulfillment of years")

As you can see, both phrases can be done in English with "for" but in Spanish, the first one has a destination to reach or an objective to accomplish, and the second sentence has an origin or reason to happen.

Han cerrado las tiendas **por** la lluvia = They have closed the shops due to (because of) the rain. The rain is the origin or reason of the action to happen. There are other cases in English where origins and destinations are expressed with FOR, but these cases can also be distinguished in Spanish using the rules.

I wait **for** him = He is the origin of my waiting process = Espero **por** él.

I wait **for** entering = Entering is the objective I reach by waiting = Espero **para** entrar.

The prepositions could be exchanged and the sentences would make sense, even if they sounded a bit strange, but the meanings would be different: "espero **por** entrar" = I wait due to entering, would mean that I entered a place and as a result now I have to wait for something to happen. We are already entering strange cases, but as you can see, they can also be tackled using the **POR / PARA** rules about origins and destinations.

Prepositions are used as in English. They usually have to precede another element, and although they can also be seen finishing a sentence, their function is to connect other elements.

Before the monument = **Ante** el monumento

In the monument = **En** el monumento

Without the monument = **Sin** el monumento

In English we form adverbs adding **-ly** (happily, sadly, slowly). In Spanish, that type of adverbs derived from other words are formed adding **-mente** or **-amente**. In general, we can say that if the word (usually an adjective) ends in **-O**, the adverb will be formed with **-AMENTE**, whereas in any other case, it's simply with **-MENTE**:

Feliz = Happy / Feliz**mente** = Happily

Triste = Sad / Triste**mente** = Sadly

Rápido = Quick / Rápid**amente** = Quickly

TRICKS TO ACQUIRE VOCABULARY

At this point there are so many new words. It might be a bit difficult to remember them all re-reading the chapters, writing them on your notebook, etc. So there are some things we can do when learning a new language to get passive vocabulary without spending too much time and energy on the effort. This is going to sound a bit crazy but bear with me...

Post-it notes... everywhere. The concept is simple. There are places in our house that we must visit very often, several times per day, so if instead of an empty cupboard door, we have a post it on it with one or two adjectives, adverbs, verbs, etc. and the translation, every time you go to that cupboard for something, you will open it and see a note reminding you of 2 words. By the end of the week you will have looked at those two words an average of 14 times (twice per day). When you are tired of looking at the same two words you learned days ago, it will be time to replace them for 2 new ones. How many places in your house or desk do you check often? If you had 6 places (2 cupboards, one shelf, the book near the TV, etc.) and you had 2 words on them, at the end of the week you would have 12 words memorized without any extra time or effort, just by brushing your teeth and seeing the same post-it note on the mirror one day, and another, and the next...

Another trick that seems to work very well is to laminate or put a plastic cover on a set of words and stick them on the shower wall. That way you can be studying while washing yourself. Instead of staring at empty tiles, the words would be there for you to check whenever you look in that direction. 6 words in an A4 paper every week would mean more than 300 extra words per year, as an added amount, without even mentioning those you can learn through studying normally or with the other post-it notes. So, crazy as it may sound, scattering vocabulary around will maximize your results without any extra effort.

Another way to activate the memory mechanisms of the brain is through association, usually through an auditory response. If you say some word or term with a special music, a funny accent or stammering on purpose, the brain recognizes automatically that there is a difference with everyday speech, so it fills a small compartment with that word. Let's imagine the word "**aparcar**" = to park. Another regular word... but if you started playing with it making machine gun sounds: "ap ap ap papapapapapapar.... CAR! Aparcar... apapapar CAR!" you would have a playful association of those noises with the word **CAR**, and it would be hard to forget that word ever again. You also have the possibility of cutting words and associating concepts instead of noises: aparcar... hmm... sounds similar to "apart - car", leaving a car apart from traffic, yes, makes sense...

Every person has a different preference for vocabulary, but I have seen impressive results in everyone who used the post-its around the house and the laminated paper for the shower. Even if you didn't want to learn on purpose, looking at the same words 27 times makes you remember them whether you like it or not.

REFLEXIVE PRONOUNS AND COMPLEMENTS

In English there is a difference between "I do something" and "something is done to me". That same difference exists in Spanish, and just as "I" and "me" or "we" and "us" are different depending on the fact that they are doing an action or receiving it, in Spanish we have the same phenomenon.

The reflexive pronouns are usually placed before the action (before the verb) although later we will see cases in which they can go also at the end of a sentence, closing it.

Me = To me
Te = To you
Le / La = To him / To her
Nos = To us
Os = To you (plural, you people, both masculine and feminine)
Les / Las = To them (masculine, and to them feminine)

Before using them and getting all mixed up, there is a way to avoid all those problems easily. The trick is to ask the following question before building a phrase: **WHO DOES THE ACTION?** and then, and only then, to determine **WHO** receives that action.

Let's imagine I buy him chocolate. I would first think of "I buy" because I am the one doing that action and then I would think of the person or people receiving the action, in this case "him"

Yo compro = I buy / Yo **le** compro chocolate = I buy him chocolate (we take away YO, as we always do because it's not necessary to understand the sentence = **le compro chocolate**)

This would be me, buying chocolate for everyone:

Me comp**ro** chocolate = I buy ME chocolate (for myself)
Te comp**ro** chocolate = I buy you chocolate
Le comp**ro** chocolate = I buy him / her chocolate
Nos comp**ro** chocolate = I buy us chocolate (yes, it sounds weird in English and Spanish, true)
Os comp**ro** chocolate = I buy you (you people) chocolate
Les comp**ro** chocolate = I buy them chocolate

As you can see, I am always the one doing the action of buying chocolate, so that part doesn't change. The recipient of the action changes with the pronoun and that's it.

Let's imagine now everyone is buying me chocolate, because I am a cool teacher and my book is awesome... The structures would be like this:

Me comp**ro** chocolate = I buy myself chocolate
Me comp**ras** chocolate = You buy me chocolate
Me comp**ra** chocolate = He buys me chocolate
Me comp**ramos** chocolate = We buy me chocolate (again, yes, this construction is weird)
Me comp**ráis** chocolate = You (you people) buy me chocolate
Me comp**ran** chocolate = They buy me chocolate

As you can see, it's just the present of the verb **comprar**, and the pronoun **me** stays the same, because all of them are buying the chocolate to me.

With this thing in mind, you probably heard the expression: "me gusta". It's usually translated as "I like..." or "I like it" (although "it" it not mentioned), but it's just for practical reasons. For grammatical reasons we are going to translate it as: "it pleases me", because it is accurate and everything will make a lot more sense that way.

Me gusta el chocolate = Chocolate pleases me

Te gusta el chocolate = Chocolate pleases you

Le gusta el chocolate = Chocolate pleases him / her

Nos gusta el chocolate = Chocolate pleases us

Os gusta el chocolate = Chocolate pleases you (you people)

Les gusta el chocolate = Chocolate pleases them

In those examples **chocolate** is doing the action of pleasing **me, you, him,** etc. So, keeping in mind the rule of finding first who does the action, it's easy to build this type of sentences.

The next element is to add "it" to the formula. "It" in Spanish has a masculine and a feminine form. **Lo** = It (masculine) / **La** = It (feminine). It would be added, as in English, in substitution of the noun (chocolate).

Te compro chocolate = I buy you chocolate

Te **lo** compro = I buy **it** to you

Nos compra la casa = He buys us the house

Nos **la** compra = He buys **it** to us

Attention: Unlike in English, in Spanish we tend to repeat the pronoun and the person receiving the action. It is not grammatically impossible not to do it, but in conversation it would be very strange to not see both elements if there is ANY DOUBT about the person receiving the action:

Le compr**o** chocolate **a Juan** = I buy chocolate to him, to Juan.

In English we can also see these repetitions or clarifications: "You people are great!" (Instead of just "you") "Give it to her... to your neighbor". But in Spanish they are much more common, so keep it in mind when building sentences:

Juan **me** compr**a** chocolate y **yo le** compr**o** chocolate **a Juan**.

Juan buys chocolate to me and I buy chocolate to him, to Juan.

A good example of that repetition in which we also see the use of **YO**. That's the type of sentence in which the personal pronouns are mentioned, because it makes it faster and clearer to understand who does what to whom. Otherwise, avoid using pronouns when building regular sentences, because the verb endings already indicate who does the action.

There is one use in which even natives have problems to determine whether to use **LE** or **LO / LA**. But since we have learned the structures in this way, we now know that we can only use

LE = as a pronoun, for masculine or feminine (**him / her**)

LO / LA = as a complement, (**IT**) for masculine or feminine.

Le compro comida (al gato) = I buy food (to the cat)

Lo compro = I buy him, as a possession (I buy the cat as my new pet)

Le regalo un libro = I give (as a present) a book to him / her

La regalo = I give **it** (some feminine noun) as a present to someone (La casa, for example)

Tengo una casa y **la** regalo = I have a house and I give **it** away (I give it as a present)

The most difficult case, is one in which natives were making so many mistakes, that the Royal Academy ended up accepting both uses as grammatically correct. Here we have already learned the difference between doing an action to "him" and "him" being part of the action (direct or indirect complement), but remember that both are accepted:

Ese es Antonio. **Le** llamo "El Magnífico" = That's Antonio. I call **him** "El Magnífico"

Ese es Antonio. **Lo** llamo "El Magnífico" = That's Antonio. I call **it** "El Magnífico"

As you can guess, the originally correct one is the first one, because Antonio is a person, not a thing. The action is done to him, he is not part of the action being done. BUT, the confusion came with the feminine case:

Le llamo un taxi a mi amiga = I call a taxi to (for) my female friend (I do something to her)

La llamo "La Magnífica" = I call her "La Magnífica" (she receives my nickname directly. She is the one receiving this call in form of a nickname, not a taxi that will later go to pick her up as in the other sentence).

It's not easy… in fact it has to be difficult if even natives make mistakes with this part, but I will be glad if you keep this rule in mind and you remember a vague explanation about this phenomenon once you start seeing examples of sentences with pronouns, reflexives, etc.

Lo siento = I am sorry (I feel it, sentir = to feel).

The reflexive pronoun SE for himself, herself, itself, themselves

What happens when he does something to himself or she does something to herself? As you can see if you check the list, Le compra, would mean that he or she buys something to another guy or girl:

Juan **le compra** agua a María = Juan buys water to María = Juan **le** compra agua.

For those cases in which he, she, it, or they, do something to themselves, we use the pronoun **SE**. And the examples would be like this:

Ana **se** lava con agua = Ana washes herself with water
Carlos **se** pierde fácilmente = Carlos loses himself easily (gets easily lost)
Ellas **se** compran cosas todos los días = They (feminine) buy themselves things every day.

As you can see, it's very simple. One pronoun substitutes the English "himself", "herself", "itself", "themselves", in Spanish. But it gets even better, because SE also substitutes the constructions in reflexive: "is done", "is played", "it is said that..."

The cake **is done** with sugar = La tarta se hace con azúcar
Football **is played** with a ball = El fútbol se juega con una pelota
It is said that eating a lot is bad = Se dice que comer mucho es malo

In the last sentence you are probably wondering where is "it" or "lo"... WRONG! How could you? Remember that in Spanish we only use "it" or "lo" as a complement, not as a pronoun. If you ever need to use the pronoun "it" in one of these constructions, we substitute it by "this" or "that" = Eso se cocina con agua = That **is cooked** with water. But mostly it is just omitted. This sentence will be useful:

¿Cómo **se dice** esa palabra en español? = How is that word said in Spanish?
¿Cómo **se dice** "platypus" en español? = How is "platypus" said in Spanish?
(not that you need it, but in case you are wondering... "platypus" is: "ornitorrinco")

In structures like the English: "**for sale**" or "**for rent**", we also see the absence of any pronoun or complement, in Spanish it's also done with "**se**":
Se vende = for sale (it is sold... as in, it is being sold by someone).
Se alquila = for rent (it is rented... as in, it is being rented by someone)

IMPORTANT: There's another type of use of **SE** that is also quite easy, but it could be mixed with the others. Whenever (and only if) we have "LE" + "LO","LA", "LOS", "LAS" (to him/her + it in singular or plural, masculine or feminine) we will change the "LE" part for "SE". That's all. It has nothing to do with "himself", "herself", etc. It doesn't alter the meaning of the sentence in any way... It's just a resource to avoid having too many L letters in those constructions.

Le compro un barco = I buy him/her a boat
Lo compro = I buy it (masculine, the boat)
Le lo compro = WRONG! :(
Se lo compro = RIGHT! :) I buy **IT** to **HIM/HER**

It's not about himself, or herself. We are just avoiding the repetition of the L in two consecutive short words.

Les doy la casa = I give them the house ("they" as in, guys or girls)
La doy = I give it (feminine, the house)
Les la doy = WRONG! :(
Se la doy = RIGHT! :) I give it to them

What if instead of one boat or one house we had 2 or 3? Same constructions as above, but instead of **LO** or **LA**, we would have **LOS** or **LAS** (plural, more than one boat or house).

Le compro unos barcos = I buy him some boats
Los compro = I buy them (the boats)
Le los compro = WRONG! :(
Se los compro = RIGHT! :) (I buy them to him)

Les doy las casas = I give the houses to them
Las doy = I give them (the houses)
Les las doy = WRONG! :(
Se las doy = RIGHT! :) I give them (the houses) to them (to those guys)

As in the other tenses and structures, usted and ustedes: "you sir / madam" "you ladies / gentlemen" is conjugated as a third person, as a he / she / they. You are so important that I can't address you directly... "May I help you sir?" = "May I help him?":

¿**Le** puedo ayudar en algo? = Can I help you, Sir, in something? (with anything)
¿**Les** puedo recomendar un restaurante? = May I recommend you, ladies and gentlemen, a restaurant?

It's a good moment to insist on the fact that we are not peasants in a 16th century colony of the New World, and the King of Spain won't hang us for not keeping enough distance with people. So, unless you are given the treatment of "**usted**" first, the safe approach is to be friendly and eliminate barriers. "May I have this dance, Miss?" is no longer the correct way to approach anyone at a club. The fact that some people (even native speakers in some Latin American countries) mistake distance for respect is only an excuse in business settings, in which you can't explain to your potential clients that they are overusing those pronouns as a constant reminder of a time in which the knight, the priest, the bishop, the mayor, the lord... didn't want to be close to you in any way. They didn't "respect" those around them, they simply kept them at a distance on purpose, which is in a way, more disrespectful in its essence than offering kindness and friendship when we meet someone new.

On the other hand, in some situations, if the person insists on addressing you as "sir" or "madam" even after you ask to be addressed normally, the only possible course of action if they refuse to be normal is to answer back also with "sir" or "madam" because of a non-written protocol habit that states that we must give the same treatment that we receive. So addressing someone as "tú" if they are on a crusade to keep using "usted" with you, would break certain protocol rules. If you are fine with that, go ahead. Otherwise, we express our preference for being addressed as "tú", we insist once or twice, then we sigh and give up, conscious of the fact that not everyone has learned these things properly.

Reflexive pronouns with other tenses

As you can imagine, the same way in which we say "I buy it to her", we can say "I will buy it to her", "I would buy it to her" "I am going to buy it to her", etc. The placing of the pronouns and complements always follows the same pattern. With the tenses we have seen so far we can also form some of these examples:

Te lo acaba de comprar = He/She has just bought it to you
Me la voy a comprar = I am going to buy it (feminine thing) to/for myself
Se lo he comprado = I have bought it to him/her/them
Nos lo compraríamos, pero no tenemos dinero = We would buy it to ourselves but we don't have money.
Os la están comprando ahora = They are buying it to you (you people) now
Se lo comprarán = They will buy it to themselves / them / her / him

As you see, when the pronoun **SE** appears, we need to be extra careful to determine the action and who receives it, because it can be for himself, herself, themselves... If we don't see the action being done by her, it can't be received by herself. If we don't see it being done by them, it can't be received by themselves. So before building or understanding a phrase, we follow the usual rule of asking: "who does the action?" and only after establishing that: "who receives it?"

In the last sentence: "Se lo comprarán", we need a context to know who is that **SE** talking about. The sentence is one of the most difficult cases, without a context, which is precisely why we clarify who receives the action most of the times:

Se lo comprarán a María y a Juan = They will buy it to them, to María and Juan.

It's also done without names, just with other pronouns, in this way:

Se lo comprarán a ellos = They will buy it to them, to them (repeating the element to clarify)

IMPORTANT: Just like in English, when the action is FOR somebody, we don't use: for I, for he, for she... We use: for me, for him, for her etc. In Spanish we only need to change two of the usual pronouns, so the list would be like this:

Para **mí** = For me
Para **ti** = For you
Para él / Para ella = For him / her
Para nosotros / Para nosotras = For us
Para vosotros / Para vosotras = For you (you people)
Para ellos / Para ellas = For them

Therefore we can make phrases in which we repeat the recipient with them, and only "me" and "you" in singular will change:

Me compras el regalo a **mí**, no a mi amigo = You buy the present to me, to me, not to my friend.
Me lo compras a **mí** = You buy it to me, to me.
Te compro el regalo a **ti**, no a tu amigo = I buy the present to you, to you, not to your friend.
Te lo compro a **ti** = I buy it to you, to you.

Finally, and to understand these pronouns totally, and in some cases better than some natives, you need to know that in **INFINITIVES, GERUNDS** and **IMPERATIVES**, you can actually choose if to add those particles in the beginning (as we have been doing) or in the end. Examples:

Quiero comprar un libro = I want to buy a book
Lo quiero comprar = I want to buy it
Quiero comprar**lo** = I want to buy it

Te quiero llamar hoy = I want to call you today
Quiero llamar**te** hoy = I want to call you today

Te lo voy a decir = I am going to tell it to you
Voy a decír**telo** = I am going to tell it to you

Estoy comprando = I am buying
Lo estoy comprando = I am buying it
Estoy comprándo**lo** = I am buying it

As you can see, with infinitives and gerunds, the position can change and the phrase still means the same. If we put it at the beginning, then the sentence goes separate, and if we put it in the end, the pronouns make one word (**comprándolo**). Why can we choose this placement in the beginning or in the end in these 2 cases? If you put it in the beginning, it's the normal way, as we have been doing it so far. There is a present, or a past, or a future and the pronoun can go there. On the other hand, to be able to put it in the end you need either an infinitive (the verb without changes... "to play", "to swim", "jug**ar**", "nad**ar**") or a gerund (the verb when it ends in **-ING** in English or **-ANDO**, **-IENDO** in Spanish). The third case in which you put it in the end is with the **IMPERATIVE AFFIRMATIVE** (do this! sit there! etc.) but we haven't seen that one yet... I just want it to ring a bell if you see something of that sort in future pages)

If you have any doubts understanding these rules, don't stress. Keep in mind that these are the rules to understand the phrases and structures you will encounter in real life. So you just need a general feeling about these things to reinforce it and see everything clear once you encounter enough examples in texts or conversation. Instead of a 100% understanding about all this, at this point you should be happy if you remember that pronouns can go in the beginning or in the end with those 3 tenses: "What is this **LO** doing here at the end? Ah! I remember something about it being in the end if there is an infinitive or a gerund... yes".

Vocabulary: The Body

Cuerpo = Body
Dedos = Fingers / Toes (same word for feet and hands)
Pies = Feet (one foot would be **PIE**, without the accent, that was removed years ago)
Rodillas = Knees
Piernas = Legs

Caderas = Hips (although the word exists, it's used considerably less than in English)

Muslos = Thighs

Cintura = Waist

Estómago = Stomach (the normal version of that body part, the one to use at the doctor)

Barriga = Belly (the informal word, to use in regular conversation)

Pecho = Chest

Pechos = Breasts (the **-S** at the end makes it plural, without it, it's chest or one breast)

Hombros = Shoulders

Brazos = Arms

Codos = Elbows

Muñecas = Wrists (it also means "dolls", it's not related, but it's interesting to remember)

Manos = Hands (despite ending in **-O** it's feminine so: **La mano / Las manos**)

Espalda = Back

Culo = Ass (don't even think about translating American expressions into Spanish. They will not make any sense whatsoever. For insults and sexual things we will have a subject later on)

Cuello = Neck

Cabeza = Head

Cara = Face

Ojos = Eyes

Nariz = Nose

Boca = Mouth

Orejas = Ears (there is a word **OIDO** for the inner ear, if someone sings badly, that's the part that hurts and gets mentioned in the sentence, not **orejas**)

Labios = Lips

Dientes = Teeth (one tooth is **diente**, without the -S)

Pestañas = Eyelashes

Cejas = Eyebrows

Frente = Forehead (literally "front" of the head, so the word is used for more things)

Piel = Skin

Pelo = Hair

Moreno = Dark (also for skin tones. "Estás moreno = You look tanned" after the beach or after going on holidays. "Eres moreno = You are tanned" as a person. Your natural skin tone is dark.

Castaño = Brown (for hair)

Rubio = Blond

Pelirrojo = Red (for hair, and we say "Pelo pelirrojo", even if the word "pelo" is repeated)

The last words are adjectives, so if we apply them to a girl, they change to -A:

Un**a** amig**a** rubi**a** = A blond girl friend / Un**os** hombr**es** castañ**os** = Some men with brown hair.

The word "moreno" can talk about hair or skin color, so the element it refers to usually gets mentioned to avoid confusion: **Un hombre de pelo moreno** = A man with dark hair. In some countries and precisely in some age ranges, the word "negro" for a black man is considered somehow insensitive, and the word "moreno" gets used instead. In a twist of language uses, now the terms have taken opposite places, and it's considered offensive not to describe a black person as "**negro / negra**", so "**moreno**" is used for brown-skinned people or white people that got tanned by the environment.

As you will learn, cultural differences make subjects regarding race and appearance vary in Hispanic countries compared to the English-speaking ones. Appearance gets a predominant position overcoming race as the element of interest or significance, which means that a red-haired man will get more attention than a black person in most areas, and this attention is due to exotic or uncommon elements, which is an inherent part of the Hispanic culture, and one of the historical reasons explaining why most families in Latin America have mixed ancestry whereas in English-speaking countries the mixing is less prevalent.

A good way to review the parts of the body is using that vocabulary to express injuries, accidents and pain, which is our next topic.

Pain / Dolor - Injuries / Heridas

The structure in English is with a possessive pronoun: "My head hurts" (the head is mine and it hurts in general). Whereas in Spanish, the structure is with a reflexive pronoun like the ones we saw. **Doler** = To hurt / **Me duele** = It hurts to me. After that, we just introduce the element with an article:

Me duele la cabeza = The head hurts to me (My head hurts, but with Spanish grammar, it becomes obvious that the head hurting me... is mine).

It might not be very clear yet, but luckily we have a construction in English that is more or less the same: "It pains me to see you cry", "It pains me to have to say this but..." In our case, we would be talking about "The head pains me", understanding that the head causing me such pain is my own. So we will be using the pronouns we already know but we only need "duele" for singular organs and "duelen" for plural.

Me duel**en** las piernas = My legs hurt
Le duel**e** la espalda = His / Her / Its back hurts
¿**Te** duel**en** lo ojos? = Do your eyes hurt?
Nos duel**en** los dientes = Our teeth hurt
Os duel**e** la cara = Your face hurts
Les duel**e** el pecho = Their chests hurt (notice how the construction in Spanish has a singular "**pecho**" instead of a plural "**pechos**" which would indicate that their **breasts** are the ones hurting, instead of the whole chest)

Of course, changing the tense will allow us to use some of the forms we already know:

Me va a doler la cabeza = My head is going to hurt
Le dolerá el estómago si come mucho helado = His / Her stomach will hurt if he / she eats a lot of ice cream (**helado** = ice cream)
Te ha dolido el hombro hasta hoy = Your shoulder has hurt you until today
Les están doliendo las piernas = Their legs are hurting

It's also worth mentioning that just like in English, my head can hurt, words can hurt, getting punched in the face can hurt, etc. So those origins of pain remain common:

Le duelen las manos = The hands hurt him (his hands hurt)
Le duelen tus **palabras** = Your words hurt him (tus palabras = your words)
Me duelen vuestras acusaciones = Your (you people) accusations hurt me

Herida = Wound
Tengo una herida en la mano y me duele = I have a wound in my hand and it hurts me

Corte = Cut
Me he cortado en la pierna y es un problema = I have cut myself "in the leg" and it's a problem.

Caerse = To Fall (me caigo, te caes, se cae, nos caemos, os caéis, se caen) It's reflexive, so I "fall myself"

A menudo cuando voy en bicicleta me caigo y me duele = Often, when I go by bicycle I fall and it hurts (a menudo = often)

Spanish Surnames / Apellidos Españoles

After all these words, a random cultural note will help us relax a bit. As you may have noticed, Spanish names are usually longer than English ones. The general explanation for this is that we use the surname of our father and the surname of our mother as the second one.

The reasons for this sink their roots in the development of Spain as a nation and then as an empire. It was important for people to know precisely who you were, what your story was, and any advantage regarding family names could be crucial in order to be accepted immediately in a new environment. People were proud of their combination of surnames because with so many wars and such a rapid growth, it was almost impossible not to have some sort of war hero or noble ancestor in your family heritage. The History of Spain is so bloody and so ingrained in conflict that it is almost a challenge to find a family in which there isn't a knighthood at the very least. Most coats of arms have military elements in them and most families mixing didn't want part of that heritage to go down the drain if they had a daughter who could, therefore, not pass the family name.

As a practical example, and purely to clarify this issue, let's imagine that the son of Stephen Hawking and the daughter of Arnold Schwarzenegger had a son named Timothy. His name, were he born in a Spanish-speaking country, would be:
Timothy Hawking Schwarzenegger
Both surnames would be part of his official name, he would sign with both, but he would only be able to pass his first surname to his children. If Timothy then married the granddaughter of Picasso and they had a son named John, he would be John Hawking Picasso.

You can see how telling your art teacher that you are the grandson of Picasso can be impressive, as well as telling your science teacher that you are also the grandson of Stephen Hawking. Well, this thing applied to 12th century Spain, 15th century Spain, the new colonies, etc. would mean that you share the feats of whatever families are present in your genealogy. "Yes, I might have arrived to the New World yesterday on a wooden boat without money, but my mother's family fought to defend the city of your father's family in some obscure battle 200 years ago and you wouldn't exist if it weren't for that, so I want a job, or at least respect in a new environment such as a newly discovered continent".

The law in the 19th century stated that only 2 surnames could be the official ones in documents, because a lot of people were too proud of their full heritage and they were using 6 or 8 family names. So all these things should be taken into consideration:

-If you check information about some historical Spanish figure and his name is too damn long, it's because he was using several of the surnames from his genealogical tree (before the 19th century).

-Women don't change their surnames when they marry in a Spanish-speaking country, they pass their surname to their children, but these will not pass it to the grandchildren.

-Anything more than those two surnames nowadays is not allowed in any country, so whatever other word is present, it will be a middle name because of the tradition of giving composed names to children, so that either both families feel included in the naming process, or the name of the child appears longer and more important.

-Although the first surname is the important one, if you have a common first surname, and an uncommon second one, you will most likely be known to people by the second one, such as with former President of Spain Jose Luis Rodríguez Zapatero, where Jose and Luis are name and middle name, Rodríguez is his dad's surname and Zapatero is his mom's surname... He was usually referred to as "Presidente Zapatero", and he even made it his personal trademark in some campaigns.

-The habit, of course, extended in the Spanish colonies even if there wasn't any practical reason to give extra information about the families composing your genealogical tree. Something like: "I have no idea about the real surnames of my ancestors. The Spaniards came, conquered these lands and gave us all Spanish-sounding surnames". Nowadays the tradition of using two surnames is total, but originally it was a way to boast about heritage and nobility.

-Nowadays nobody gives much importance to surnames, although it is always more recognizable to see a combination of uncommon Spanish surnames than to, for example, create a character for a novel called: "Manuel López Rodríguez", which could literally be anyone, born anywhere, whose families aren't particularly recognizable or associated with any historical episode or geographical area.

The clothes : La ropa

Keep in mind that these words vary a lot from country to country and even from region to region, so we will only learn the common terms used in the shops and online stores.

Zapatos = Shoes

Botas = Boots

Zapatillas = Slippers

Zapatillas de deporte = Trainers / Snickers (literally "sport slippers")

Chanclas = flip-flops

Calcetines = socks

Medias = Stockings

Pantalón / Pantalones = Trousers (generic ones go usually in plural)

Falda = Skirt

Vestido = Dress

Calzoncillos = Briefs

Braguitas = Panties

Bañador = Swimsuit

Bikini = Bikini

Camisa = Shirt

Camiseta = T-shirt

Blusa = Blouse

Jersey = Sweater / Jumper

Chaqueta = Jacket (any type of jacket, like in English)

Cinturón = Belt

Chaleco = Vest

Abrigo = Coat

Sujetador = Bra

Gorro = Hat

Sombrero = Hat with a brim

Gorra = Cap

Bufanda = Scarf

Guantes = Gloves

Collar = Necklace

Pendientes = Earrings

The word **pantalones** is generic, and gets used in plural more often than in singular:
I have bought myself some trousers = Me he comprado unos pantalones

However, when the trousers are specific for an activity, the word gets used in singular more often than in plural, **pantalón**:
Me he comprado un pantalón de deporte y un pantalón de esquí = I have bought myself some sport trousers and some skiing trousers.

As in many other cases, the word **jersey** in Spanish is something someone got wrong. A word that was brought to the Spanish language meaning something different from the original. In English, the thickness of this clothing item is less than in Spanish. Another good example of words that became international without people fully grasping the meaning is the term "**ticket**". In Spanish you get that piece of paper after a purchase, as a receipt. And you don't get a parking ticket, you kind of get a "parking penalty" or "parking fine" which is called a **multa**.

Some verbs that we need to know include:

Vestirse = To dress (me visto, te vistes, se viste, nos vestimos, os vestís, se visten) It has to be reflexive because we can also put clothes on a kid, a doll; a butler could dress us at some point in history, etc. Therefore, the language evolved assuming that the word needed that distinction of: "hey... I am dressing myself".

Probarse= To try on (me pruego, te pruebas, se prueba, nos probamos, os probáis, se prueban) If you use it without the particle **-SE** at the end, it will mean "to try" as in "to try food" "to try a new thing", whereas with **-SE** it becomes "to try something on myself" generally applied to clothes and complements: Voy a probarme unos pendientes = I am going to try some earrings. Quiero **probar** este helado = I want to try this ice cream

Ponerse= To put on (me pongo, te pones, se pone, nos ponemos, os ponéis, se ponen). As you know, **PONER** alone means "to put", therefore if we add **-SE** means "to put on oneself" or "to try on". Tengo frío... voy a ponerme una chaqueta = I am cold... I am going to put on a jacket.

As you can see, in Spanish we express cold or warmth with the verb **TENER** (to have) so it literally means "I have cold". **Tengo calor** = I am warm (I have warmth)

That is when I am the one who is cold, but when cold is general, for example, when it's cold outside, we use the verb **HACER** = To make. Usually in the third person: it makes cold. What is it? the weather, the environment produces cold, reality makes cold for us to feel it... As you can see this is partly what they mean when they mention that learning a new language changes your views on things: "The environment makes it cold for us!"

Hace frío = It's cold
Tengo frío = I am cold
Hace calor = It's warm
Tengo calor = I am warm
Hace viento = It's windy (it makes wind)

Although this is so, keep in mind that some meteorological processes have their own verbs, just like in English. It's raining = Está llov**iendo** / It's snowing = Está nev**ando**
Llover = To rain / Hoy llueve en Galicia = Today it rains in Galicia
Nevar = To snow / Mañana nevará en Madrid = Tomorrow it will snow in Madrid

PRACTICE PHRASES

(write down the new words on your notebook to remember them)

Me gustaría escribir algo en español para que puedas ver que ahora es muy fácil saber cómo usar las palabras. I would like to write something so that you can see that now it's very easy to know how to use the words.

En unas semanas podrás leer textos difíciles y comprender todo. In some weeks you will be able to read difficult texts and understand everything.

Mi amigo tiene una tienda en Madrid y siempre me llama cuando está aburrido. My friend has a shop in Madrid and he always calls me when he is bored.

Siempre hablamos de viajes y de los sitios a los que nos gustaría ir. We always talk about trips and about the places to which we would like to go.

En el futuro viajaré a muchos sitios interesantes y podré hacer fotos en varios países. In the future I will go to many interesting places and I will be able to "do photos (take photos)" in several countries.

¿No te gustaría ir conmigo de viaje y conocer lugares nuevos? Wouldn't you like to go with me "on" a trip and know new places?

He estado viviendo en algunas ciudades de países diferentes y siempre aprendo algo nuevo. I have been living in some cities "of" different countries and I always learn something new.

Estoy pensando que es muy tarde y debería dormir. I am thinking that it's very late and I should sleep (deber = must, debería = should).

Mañana por la mañana iré al banco a arreglar unos papeles. Tomorrow in the morning (yes, the word "mañana" is used both for tomorrow and for morning) I will go to the bank to fix some papers (arreglar = to fix / to mend).

¿Puedes venir conmigo para ayudarme después con una cosa? Can you come with me to help me afterwards with a thing?

No sé si sabes que esta semana es el cumpleaños de Fernando y tenemos que comprarle un regalo. I don't know if you know that this week is the birthday of Fernando and we have to buy him a present.

Yo nunca sé qué comprar, por eso me gustaría ir juntos y elegir algo entre los dos. I never know what to buy, for this (that's why) I would like to go together (juntos=together) and choose something between the two (the two of us).

Si quieres podemos preguntarle a su mujer para ver si ella sabe qué le puede gustar. If you want we can ask his wife to see if she knows what he can like (a perfect example of a time where the pronoun is needed to make it clear that SHE and not HE is the one mentioned) (mujer = woman / wife).

¿No crees que un libro sobre historia es un buen regalo para él? Le gusta mucho leer. Don't you think a book about history is a good gift for him? He likes a lot to read (creer = to believe, but it's used in opinions like in classical English: I believe you are right).

Podría ser... pero es muy difícil saber qué temas le interesan. ¿Quizás es mejor regalarle algo para hacer deporte? It could be... but it's very difficult to know what subjects interest him (are interesting to him). Perhaps it's better to "gift him" something to do sport? (Regalar = To give as a present)

No lo sé... De verdad que no sé qué regalarle a este hombre... I don't know it... I really don't know what "to gift" to this man. (No lo sé = I don't know it / No sé = I don't know -in general-) Verdad means "truth", and the construction "de verdad" means literally "in truth" but it is used as a "really" or "for real". ¿El coche es para mí? ¿De verdad? = The car is for me? For real?

PAST TENSES: IMPERFECTO AND PERFECTO (I was eating / I ate)

The title of this part says it all. There are two pasts in Spanish that are equivalent to a simple past (I cooked) and to a past continuous (I was cooking). Just like in English, the first one is shorter and it talks about a simple action happening in the past (I cooked... that's it...) The second one is longer to write or say and it talks about a process (I was cooking... when my friend called) In "I cooked" I can't introduce other actions because it's not a process. In "I was cooking" I can put other things happening in the past because it's a process: "I was cooking when I received a called, I spoke for 5 minutes, then I poured some water in a glass anddddd went on cooking".

Pasado Imperfecto (A.K.A. Pretérito Imperfecto de Indicativo)

Verbs ending in **-AR** like **NADAR**

Yo Nad**aba** = I was swimming
Tú Nad**abas** = You were swimming
Él / Ella / Usted Nad**aba** = He / She / You Sir - Madam was swimming
Nosotros / Nosotras Nad**ábamos** = We were swimming

Vosotros / Vosotras Nad**abais** = You (you people) were swimming

Ellos / Ellas / Ustedes Nad**aban** = They / You ladies - gentlemen were swimming

Verbs ending in **-ER** like **COMER** or ending in **-IR** like **VIVIR** (they have the same endings)

Yo Com**ía** = I was eating

Tú Com**ías** = You were eating

Él / Ella / Usted Com**ía** = He / She / You Sir - Madam was eating

Nosotros / Nosotras Com**íamos** = We were eating

Vosotros / Vosotras Com**íais** = You (you people) were eating

Ellos / Ellas / Ustedes Com**ían** = They / You ladies - gentlemen were eating

Yo Viv**ía** = I was living

Tú Viv**ías** = You were living

El / Ella / Usted Viv**ía** = He / She / You Sir - Madam was living

Nosotros / Nosotras Viv**íamos** = We were living

Vosotros / Vosotras Viv**íais** = You (you people) were living

Ellos / Ellas / Ustedes Viv**ían** = They / You ladies - gentlemen were living

A good way to remember this past is to memorize the endings for -AR in some sort of song or accent that you don't usually use:

-aba / -abas / -aba / -ábamos / -abais / -aban

And then the ones for -ER and -IR in another song or funny voice for the same reason. Your brain will make an association and you will not mix this past with others, because this is the past of the strange songs and voices to remember the endings:

-ía / -ías / -ía / -íamos / -íais / -ían

The simple past is shorter, and it has less letters (important fact for later). It's called:

Pasado Perfecto Simple (A.K.A. Pretétiro Perfecto Simple de Indicativo)

Verbs ending in **-AR** like **NADAR**

Yo Nad**é** = I swam

Tú Nad**aste** = You swam

Él / Ella / Ustéd Nad**ó** = He / She / You Sir - Madam swam

Nosotros / Nosotras Nad**amos** = We swam

Vosotros / Vosotras Nad**asteis** = You (you people) swam

Ellos / Ellas / Ustedes Nad**aron** = They / You ladies - gentlemen swam

Verbs ending in **-ER** like **COMER** or ending in **-IR** like **VIVIR** (they have the same endings)

Yo Com**í** = I ate

Tú Com**iste** = You ate

Él / Ella / Usted Com**ió** = He / She / You Sir - Madam ate

Nosotros / Nosotras Com**imos** = We ate

Vosotros / Vosotras Com**isteis** = You (you people) ate

Ellos / Ellas / Ustedes Com**ieron** = They / You ladies - gentlemen ate

Yo Viv**í** = I lived

Tú Viv**iste** = You lived

Él / Ella / Usted Viv**ió** = He / She / You Sir - Madam lived

Nosotros / Nosotras Viv**imos** = We lived

Vosotros / vosotras Viv**isteis** = You (you people) lived

Ellos / Ellas / Ustedes Viv**ieron** = They / You ladies - gentlemen lived

As you can see, the endings of **nosotros** for verbs ending in **-AR** and **-IR** coincide with the present tense. Therefore, unless the context makes it clear, we usually add time adverbs to make it perfectly clear that we are talking either in past or in present:

Hoy **nadamos** con Alberto en su piscina = Today we **swim** with Alberto in his swimming pool

Ayer **nadamos** con Ana en el mar = Yesterday we **swam** with Ana in the sea

In the same way, yo vivía and él vivía (I was living and he was living) also coincide in the endings. The general use is to understand that unless the context points otherwise, I am talking about myself. If I mention another person and use it in the sentence I will have to clarify it with pronouns:

Yo **vivía** en Madrid y ella **vivía** en Toledo. Nos **conocimos** en un viaje
I was living in Madrid and she was living in Toledo. We met at a trip
(Conocerse = To know each other / To meet)

When to use one past and when to use the second?

The difference is just like in English. I was swimming and I saw. I was eating and I ate. For a process we will use the long one, and for a simple action happening in the past we will use the simple past.

When **I was swimming** my friend **called** me
Cuando **nadaba** mi amigo me **llamó**

In the middle of that swimming process, that went on and on, a simple past action happened (the call I received). Therefore we can see that from a philological perspective, in a pretérito imperfecto (nadaba.... the long one of the two pasts... the "I was swimming" one) we can introduce other past actions.

When **I was swimming** I **thought** about my job, I **saw** a fish, and I **received** a call
Cuando **nadaba pensé** sobre mi trabajo, **ví** un pez y **recibí** una llamada.

As you can see, I did all those other things while swimming. In that swimming timeline other simple past actions were placed. So inside a timeline of pretérito imperfecto (the long one) we can put other simple past actions with pretérito perfecto simple (the short one, the "I ate, I slept, I saw" one). But inside those small short simple past actions it's hard, not to say impossible, to place other processes or past actions. While I was swimming I did other stuff, "while I swam" I did nothing because it already sounds weird to the average speaker, and in Spanish it sounds just as weird, if not more. It is not totally impossible to introduce other simple past actions inside another simple past action, it is just specific and uncommon. One good example is the simple past of "to stand": While **I stood** there **I saw** many things (instead of "while I was standing there").

So even though those cases are possible and exist. The best trick to not mix these two pasts in Spanish is to remember that the long past (imperfecto / nad**aba** / com**ía** / viv**ía**) is a timeline in which simple pasts can be put (the short past / perfecto simple / nad**é** / com**í** / viv**í**) like this:

Cuando **comía** en el restaurante   ---
ví a mi amigo -----   **llamé** a mi hermano -----   y **pagué** la comida -----

When **I was eating** at the restaurant ---
I **saw** mi friend -----   I **called** my brother -----   and I **paid** the food -----

So those short timelines enter easily inside the big one. All of those things happened while I was eating at the restaurant

-- **Imperfecto** Timeline
-----   -----   -----   **Perfecto** Timelines

Can one of those **imperfecto** timelines also hold **imperfecto** actions? Yes. Just like in English: "while I was waiting at the dentist I was hearing the drill" during that process of waiting there, the process of hearing the drill all that time as a constant was happening.

There are a few things to consider about the examples we used before. The verb "to see" is **VER**, so to form the past, as always, we take away the ending **-ER**, and we add the endings. In this case it turns out that the verb without **-ER** is only one letter, and the ending we need is another letter, so the result is **VÍ** = I saw.

Un **pez** = a fish   / Dos **peces** = two fish / **Pescado** = Fish (as food, not alive)
Pagar = To pay (**pagué** = I payed)
Recibir = To receive (**recibí** = I received)

Sometimes if you translate something from Spanish into English it will seem that it doesn't make sense. Verbs like CAN don't have a proper simple past, or a proper participle... instead we use the form "could" from the conditional to fill those gaps. It's an irregularity in English that won't be present in Spanish. In other cases we will need to forget the habit of using a word and go to the grammatical roots for common ground. Was I nervous? Or was I being nervous? Habit will not help us whenever we are building phrases in other languages, but stopping to think about whether this action was done or was being done as a process might help us do better than most other speakers at this level.

So whenever we have to choose between defining something as a simple past action or a process happening in the past (I ate / I was eating) we need to consider that philological aspect as a first step, and then we must be patient because just like English has irregularities and things that don't make much sense for someone learning it, Spanish also has idiomatic habits and examples in which we will say: "I can clearly see that this is a process and needs an **imperfecto**... but someone in the 17th century started saying it wrong and people followed until it became the idiomatic rule... I am grammatically right, but in the end I have to communicate with other speakers, so idiomatic uses trump grammatical coherence". A good example to relate would be the use of "good" and "well". Technically we should say "I feel well" (because it's an adverb) but 90% of the time we will hear "I feel good"... there are even songs about it.

Examples of Pretérito Imperfecto and Pretérito Perfecto Simple

Mi amigo **vivía** en Salamanca cuando **conoció** a su mujer.
My friend **was living** in Salamanca when he **met** his wife.

Leí ese libro mientras **estudiaba** en la universidad.
I **read** that book while I **was studying** at the university.

No te **llamé** porque **estaba** ocupado.
I **didn't call** you because I **was** busy ("I was being busy").

Cuando **viajábamos** por Galicia **vimos** sitios muy bonitos.
When we **were traveling** around (by) Galicia, we **saw** very beautiful places.

Si **pensabas** eso... ¿Por qué no me lo **dijiste**?
If you **were thinking** that... Why **didn't you tell** me? (tell it to me)

Cuando **vivía** en España **hablaba** español todo el tiempo.
When I **was living** in Spain I **was speaking** Spanish all the time.

No **teníamos** elección. Solo **podíamos** esperar.
We had (**were having**) no choice. We could ("**were being able**") only (to) wait.

Antes **visitabais** más sitios que ahora. ¿Qué **visteis** ayer?
Before you **were visiting** more places than now. What **did you see** yesterday?

Mientras **esperaba** a mi amigo, le **escribí** un mensaje.
While **I was waiting** (to) my friend, I **wrote** him a message.

Antes **comía** muchos dulces, pero ahora como menos.
Before **I was eating** many sweets, but now I eat less.

Cuando **visité** en Malaga **bebí** vino local y **me gustó**.
When I **visited** Malaga I **drank** local wine and **I liked it**.

Hace un año **empecé** a ver películas españolas y **descubrí** que me gustaban.
A year ago I **started** to watch Spanish movies and I **discovered** that I liked them.

As you went through this subject you probably wondered at some point (or will wonder now) if you can actually translate literally the words in "I was eating" using the verb "to be". We have already seen that present continuous "I am eating" = **estoy comiendo**. The answer is YES. You can put that verb **estar** in **imperfecto** and keep the gerund making something like:
Estaba comiendo. At this level you don't need to worry about the cases in which we use one or the other. Keep in mind that this is the basic level and there are people at the advanced level still making mistakes when choosing one or the other. The only thing you need to know now is that the thing exists and it will require a chapter on its own in the future. It should be enough to remember that in a timeline where I plan to introduce other actions we use the imperfecto in the way we have learned, and if I simply answer a question or start the phrase with that process without adverbs, the form of estaba + gerund is more common.

Cuando **comía ví** un coche en la calle = When **I was eating I saw** a car on the street.
-¿Qué **hacías**? -¡Oh! **Estaba comiendo** = -What **were you doing**? -Oh! **I was eating**.

As I said, don't even stress about this sort of thing yet. There are university professors of Spanish out there who still mix both cases. We will come back to it at a later time and it will be easier to get it. Something similar to explaining in English the differences between:
"I behaved like a fool with you / I have been behaving like a fool with you / I was behaving like a fool with you / I have behaved like a fool with you". It will be much easier when your knowledge of tenses is advanced than at this point.

Irregular verbs in Imperfecto and Perfecto de Indicativo

There are irregular verbs, but the good news is that the main ones are always the same and you will see them often, so it's easy to remember them. Be careful with the verb TO BE, since in English sometimes the past "WAS" acts as imperfecto and perfecto. If you ever doubt with one to use, ask yourself: "was I happy and that's it, or was I being happy as a continuous process?" "I was the champion that year / while I was being the champion, journalists interviewed me". So most of the times both sentences wil have just "was the champion", which doesn't happen in Spanish, so we have to dig a bit deeper.

Keep in mind that ESTAR is regular in imperfecto= (yo estaba, tú estabas, él / ella / usted estaba, nosotros estábamos, etc.) but irregular in perfecto. In imperfecto we will only see two verbs. Most of the irregular ones are in perfecto de indicativo (I did, I went, I played...)

-Imperfecto de Indicativo:

SER = yo **era**, tú **eras**, él / ella / usted **era**, nosotros **éramos**, vosotros **erais**, ellos / ustedes **eran** (I was being, you were being, he was being...) Usually used only as a simple **WAS**.

IR = yo **iba**, tu **ibas**, él / ella /usted **iba**, nosotros **íbamos**, vosotros **ibais**, ellos / ustedes **iban** (I was going, you were going, he was going...)

-Perfecto de Indicativo:

ESTAR (I was, you were...)= yo est**uve**, tú est**uviste**, él / ella / usted est**uvo**, nosotros est**uvimos**, vosotros est**uvisteis**, ellos / ustedes est**uvieron**

TENER (I had, you had...)= yo t**uve**, tú t**uviste**, él / ella / usted t**uvo**, nosotros t**uvimos**, vosotros t**uvisteis**, ellos t**uvieron**

ANDAR (I walked, you walked...)= yo and**uve**, tú and**uviste**, él / ella / usted and**uvo**, nosotros and**uvimos**, vosotros and**uvisteis**, ellos and**uvieron**

CONDUCIR (I drove, you drove...)= yo condu**je**, tú condu**jiste**, él / ella / usted condu**jo**, nosotros condu**jimos**, vosotros condu**jisteis**, ellos condu**jeron**

TRAER (I brought, you brought...)= yo tra**je**, tú tra**jiste**, él / ella / usted tra**jo**, nosotros tra**jimos**, vosotros tra**jisteis**, ellos / ustedes tra**jeron**

HACER (I did, you did...)= yo **hice**, tú **hiciste**, él / ella / usted **hizo**, nosotros **hicimos**, vosotros **hicisteis**, ellos / ustedes **hicieron**

SABER (I knew, you knew...) = yo **supe**, tú **supiste**, él / usted **supo**, nosotros **supimos**, vosotros **supisteis**, ellos **supieron**

As you can see, even the irregulars follow similar patterns. The verb andar, tener and estar have literally the same endings between them, so even the irregulars have logic and patterns even if they differ from the general conjugation. As soon as you recognize these verbs, you will remember that they are conjugated in a certain way that tends to repeat. The same thing happens with conducir, traer... and for example traducir = to translate. You could just make the simple past (or pretérito perfecto simple de indicativo, the short one) with the endings from traer or conducir: yo trad**uje**, tu tradu**jiste**, él / ella / usted tradu**jo**...

Examples:

Mi amigo se **hizo** una casa en Cádiz = My friend made himself a house in Cádiz
Nunca **supe** como cocinar marisco = I never knew how to cook seafood
Le **traje** un regalo a tu hija = I brought a present to your daughter
El lunes **anduvimos** 6 kilómetros = On Monday we walked 6 kilometers
Los dos **tuvieron** problemas para aparcar = Both had problems to park
Ana **condujo** toda la noche = Ana drove all night

-The curious case of SER / IR-

In simple past (or perfecto de indicativo) these two verbs coincide. They are conjugated in the same way, so we need to differentiate them by the context. It only happens with this particular tense, because for all the rest everything is different. But in simple past the conjugation of both verbs will be like this:

yo **fui** = I went / I was
tú **fuiste** = you went / you were
él / ella / usted **fue** = he / she / you sir-madam went / were
nosotros **fuimos** = we went / we were
vosotros **fuisteis** = you (you people) went / were
ellos / ustedes **fueron** = they / you ladies-gentlemen went / were

Fui a Santiago y me gustó la comida = I went to Santiago and I liked the food
Fui fan de la opera, pero ya no = I was a fan of the opera, but now not (not anymore)
Mi primo **fue** a una fiesta = My cousin went to a party
Mi primo **fue** policía, ahora es profesor = My cousin was a policeman, now he is a teacher

Ayer **fuimos** a un bar = Yesterday we went to a bar

Ayer **fuimos** los mejores del partido = Yesterday we were the best of the match

It's easy to see the difference once we get the context. If we go to a place or we just were something in the past. Now the next important point is to know when to use:

ERA (I was --------------------) and when to use **FUI** (I was -----). As we have mentioned several times, English doesn't have a clear separation nowadays between those two concepts, so the quickest trick when you are building phrases by yourself is to change the verb to something similar. To be, changed for... "to exist" for example.

Cuando Abraham Lincoln **ERA** presidente, empezó una guerra

When Abraham Lincoln was (**was existing** / was working as) president, a war started

Abraham Lincoln **FUE** el 16º presidente de Estados Unidos

Abraham Lincoln was (**existed** / worked as the) 16th president of the U.S.

Now everything becomes clearer. He worked as president, boom! That's it. While he was working as president stuff happened, during this long time line. I don't expect you to get all this stuff perfectly, after all, this is the basic level of Spanish, and believe me, there are non-native lecturers of Spanish making mistakes about this still. I just want you to have a general idea about the separation of that **WAS** into two temporal concepts depending if the thing simply "existed" or "was existing" in a long time line.

The other pair that can present some difficulties are estaba and estuvo, but if we go back to the basics of SER and ESTAR, you will remember that ESTAR is for things that change according to the speaker and for locations. As always, WAS presents problems translated as SER and also translated as ESTAR, so let's repeat the trick from before and change that WAS for another verb to have a clearer result of the meaning we convey. Let's use "participate" or "take part". So it becomes easy when we keep that in mind:

Mi abuelo **estuvo** en la guerra.
My grandfather **was** in the war / My grandfather **participated** in the war/ My grandfather **took part** in the war.

Cuando mi abuelo **estaba** en la guerra compró una casa.
When my grandfather **was** in the war / When my grandfather **was participating in** the war / When my grandfather **was taking part in** the war he bought a house.

A couple more examples correctly translated using WAS and with other verbs to fully grasp the concept in Spanish:

-El sábado **fui** a una fiesta que **estuvo** muy bien
On Saturday I **went** to a party that **was** very well
"On Saturday I **visited** a party that **developed** very well"

-Cuando **estaba** en la fiesta vi a una chica que **era** famosa hace años
When I **was** at the party I saw a girl who **was** famous years ago
"When I **was assisting** to that party I saw a girl who **was having** fame years ago"

-Cuando **iba** al baño, mi amigo me la presentó. **Fue** una fiesta perfecta.
-When I **was going** to the bathroom, my friend introduced her to me. It **was** a perfect party.
"When I **was heading** for the bathroom, my friend introduced her to me. It **resulted in** a perfect party"

Sometimes the tenses can be changed and the sentence will still make sense, although with a slightly different meaning. Just like in English we can say: "I was going there a couple of times" and "I went there a couple of times" with small changes in the meaning, but an overall information of having gone somewhere in the past. In Spanish sometimes we can doubt between imperfecto and perfecto because both tenses might convey the right meaning, with the slight difference of the time line being long (imperfecto) or short (perfecto), the latter for simple past actions that are not elaborate.

THE FOOD AND COOKING / LA COMIDA Y COCINAR

Desayuno = Breakfast (Desayunar = To have breakfast)
Comida = Lunch (Comer = To eat, and talking about meals, to have lunch)
Merienda = Mid-afternoon snack (usually for children and old people, the verb= Merendar)
Cena = Dinner (as in: the last meal of the day / Cenar = to have dinner)
Cubiertos = Cutlery (but also "service" as in: "bring a service to another guest!"
Tenedor = Fork
Cuchillo = Knife

Cuchara = Spoon

Cucharilla = Teaspoon (cucharita is also an acceptable version. Both words are international)

Plato = Plate (and also dish / course. Primer plato = first course)

Vaso = Glass

Taza = Mug (also cup)

Mantel = Mantel piece (the big one, the small ones...)

Servilleta = Napkins

Sartén = Frying pan

Pota = Pot

Horno = Oven (Hornear = to bake, to put something in the oven, generally sweet)

Freir = To Fry

Cocer = To Boil

Asar = To Roast

Mezclar = To Mix

Echar = To Throw (and in some cases "To pour")

Batir = To Beat / To whisk (as in, beat eggs, whisk eggs)

Pelar = To Peel

Cortar = To Cut

Picar = To Mince

Remover = To stir

Enfriar = To make something cold

Calentar = To make something warm

By the words we have here, and the use of the reflexives that we already saw, you can see that I am preparing the grounds for you to understand and make recipes. So if you think about it, you could actually understand Spanish and Latin American cuisine already now, but for this we first need the ingredients you will be seeing, and the food you will be ordering at restaurants.

Leche = Milk (be careful if it has an adjective next to it; it could mean another ingredient)

Huevos = Eggs (yema = yolk / clara = white)

Azúcar = Sugar

Sal = Salt

Pan = Bread

Miel = Honey

Harina = Flour

Nata = Cream (as in whipped cream)

Queso = Cheese

Carne = Meat

Pescado = Fish

Marisco = Seafood

Postre = Dessert

Tarta = Pie

Pastel = Cake

Tapas = Small portions of food served usually with drinks, small appetizers

Entremeses = Appetizers (the regular ones at a restaurant, not a bar)

Sopa = Soup

Caldo = Stew

Pollo = Chicken

Ternera = Beef

Cerdo = Pork (and pig; the animal is called in the same way)

Atún = Tuna

Verduras = Vegetables

Patatas = Potatoes

Zanahoria = Carrot

Tomate = Tomato

Lechuga = Lettuce

Ensalada = Salad

Arroz = Rice

Aceite = Oil

Mantequilla = Butter

Fruta = Fruit

Manzana = Apple

Naranja = Naranja

Plátano = Banana (the word "banana" is also used in Spanish, but they are a bit bigger)

Uvas = Grapes

Fresas = Strawberries

Cerezas = Cherries

Melocotón = Peach

Salsa = Sauce

Zumo = Juice

Café = Coffee

Bollos = Buns

Galletas = Cookies / Biscuits

Tostada = Toast

Frutos secos = Nuts (in general: peanuts, almonds, sunflower seeds, etc.)

Cereales = Cereals

Avena = Oats

Trigo = Wheat

Maíz = Corn

RECETAS / RECIPES

-Flan de huevo-

Para esta receta los ingredientes que necesitas son: 6 huevos grandes, 250 gramos de azúcar, 1 litro de leche, la piel de un limón y esencia de vainilla.

For this recipe the ingredients you need are: 6 big eggs, 250 grams of sugar, 1 liter of milk, the skin of a lemon, and vanilla essence.

Se baten cuatro de los seis huevos en un plato, en los otros dos huevos se separan las yemas y se echan con los otros huevos. Se echa el azúcar en la mezcla y se pone la leche a calentar en una pota.

4 of the 6 eggs are whisked in a plate, with the other two eggs the yolks are separated and put (poured) with the other eggs. The sugar is thrown into the mix and the milk is put to warm in a pot.

Después de eso, echamos los huevos y el azúcar en la leche y removemos todo lentamente. Alguna gente pone la pota con la mezcla dentro de otra pota con agua caliente, para que el flan se haga bien por todos lados. También es posible echar azúcar en una pota o un vaso y calentarlo para hacer caramelo.

After that, we put the eggs and the sugar in the milk and we stir everything slowly. Some people put the pot with the mixture inside another pot with hot water so that the flan is well done by all sides. It is also possible to put sugar in a pot or a glass and warm it to make caramel.

El flan debe estar al fuego durante 1 hora y cubierto (cubrir = to cover), y para ver si está preparado, podemos introducir ligeramente un tenedor y comprobar la textura.

The flan must be on the fire during one 1 hour and covered, and to see if it's ready, we can introduce a fork slightly and check (comprobar = check) the texture.

-Pollo asado con patatas y verduras-

Esta receta es muy fácil. Se compra un pollo de unos 2 kilos, verduras variadas y patatas. Se pelan las verduras y las patatas y se cortan en trozos pequeños.

This recipe is very easy. A chicken of some 2 kilos is bought, varied vegetables and potatoes. The vegetables and the potatoes are peeled and cut in small pieces (trozo = piece).

Se quita la piel del pollo, se le echa aceite, sal, especias y se hacen cortes con un cuchillo. Así el pollo se cocinará más rápido. Se ponen las verduras y las patatas alrededor del pollo y se les echa aceite de oliva y sal. Horneamos todo a 220 ºC y esperamos 1 hora y media.

The skin of the chicken is removed. Oil, salt and spices are put and we make (are made) cuts with a knife. Like this the chicken will be cooked faster. We put (are put also possible) the vegetables and the potatoes around the chicken and we pour olive oil and salt (olive oil and salt are poured is also a valid translation, even though salt is not a liquid). We bake (roast in this case) everything at 220 degrees Celsius and we wait for one hour and a half (media = half)

-Mousse de Chocolate -

Necesitaremos 500 gramos de chocolate negro, 100 gramos de chocolate con leche, 6 huevos, 150 gramos de mantequilla y 50 gramos de frutos secos picados. Se rompe el chocolate en trozos y se pone en una pota con un poco de agua. Luego se añade la mantequilla y se remueve todo mientras el fuego covierte el chocolate en líquido. Se separan los huevos en claras y yemas y se añaden las yemas a la mezcla con los frutos secos, luego se baten las claras para hacer espuma y se añaden a la mezcla también. Se saca el mousse del fuego y se pone en tazas para enfriarlo, luego irá a la nevera durante dos horas o hasta que esté frío para comerlo con más gente.

We will need 500 grams of dark chocolate, 100 grams of milk chocolate, 6 eggs, 150 grams of butter and 50 grams of minced nuts. We break the chocolate (the chocolate is broken) in pieces and it is put in a pot with a bit of water. Then we add the butter and everything is stirred while the fire chocolate liquid. We separate the eggs into yolks and whites and we add the yolks to the mixture with the nuts, then the whites are beat to make foam (espuma = foam) and they are added to the mixture as well. We take the mousse out of the fire and we put it in cups to cool it down, then it will go to the fridge (nevera = fridge) during two hours or until it is cold to eat it with more people.

Some of the words used should be on your notebook or in notes to remember everything in an easier way. Writing will also help you familiarize with the terms and the way to write them. The translations from both recipes vary when we see "**se ponen**" "**se cortan**" "**se echan**", because we need to get used to translate those reflexive and passive constructions as "we do the action" in contexts in which it makes sense to do so.

THERE IS, THERE WAS, THERE WILL BE…

As you probably remember the verb **HABER** is the auxiliary that we used pages and pages ago to form the present perfect in Spanish (pretérito perfecto simple).

He comido = I have eaten / **Han** hablado = They have spoken / **Has** vivido = You have lived

The verb also has a peculiar form, called: "forma impersonal", that doesn't have a fixed subject. **HAY** = There is / There are. The fact of it being impersonal is important because in many countries and even in eastern parts of Spain where they have interferences from their regional languages and dialects, some people pluralize this form, which is a huge mistake that we will not be making.

The form **HAY** is for the present (there is, there are, it exists…), and the rest of the forms (there will be, there was, there have been…) are conjugated IN SINGULAR for all the cases. It's a very important rule to remember. Keep in mind that not all of the forms are easy to translate in English, but you can get the logic of their uses in Spanish. The conjugations of **hay** are the following:

Hay = There is / There are

Había = There was / There were (long time line, "there was being a war in 1872" if it could be expressed like that)

Habrá = There will be (here you can see in future, English and Spanish coincide to use singular and plural with the same form. There will be one car / There will be two cars)

Hubo = There was / There were (short time line, there was a problem and that's it. No actions in the middle of that time line)

Habría = There would be

Ha Habido = There has been / There have been

Va a haber = There is going to be / There are going to be

Está habiendo = "There is being" / "There are being" (grammatically incorrect in English, but you get the reasoning behind it for Spanish) Está habiendo muchas fiestas estos días = "There are being a lot of parties these days".

Habiendo = "There being" Habiendo salud, el resto no importa = There being health, the rest is not important. The English form is not wrong, but it is extremely limited in its use, so remember that in Spanish it is a bit more common.

Some of these forms are also used to express need or obligation in the following way:
Hay que comprar agua = There is the need to buy water
Habría que llamar a Juan = There would be the obligation to call Juan
Va a haber que dormir menos = There is going to be the need to sleep less

I know that it sounds twisted and weird, but if you think of the English contraction "gotta", you get the same feeling that a lot of elements are missing from that one too.
"Gotta buy water" = You have got to buy water = There is the need or obligation to buy water.
In Spanish **HAY QUE...** followed by the verb in infinitive (the normal one, not conjugated) expresses the same need / obligation / requirement that a "gotta" but it's not a contraction of any kind, it's just a way of saying "there exists the need or requirement of..."

Hay que tener cuidado = "**Gotta** be careful"

So it becomes impersonal. Who has to be careful? Me? You? She? **ONE** has to be careful.
"Gotta be careful these days" lacks a subject, just like it happens with the constructions of **HAY**

and the conjugations. Therefore, and this is important, we use this type of resource to give unsolicited advice, to debate or present our ideas as if they were facts accepted by society instead of mere opinions. "**Hay que** comer bien" = "**Gotta** eat well" / "**One has to** eat well" / "**There is the need** to eat well". Where is that sacred law written? Can't I spoil my health if it pleases me? Is it a moral obligation? Debatable as it may be, these impersonal constructions avoid sounding paternalistic, condescending or too intrusive imposing our opinions as in: "¡Tienes que comer bien!" = "You have to eat well!". That literally sounds like a direct order.

Examples of sentences with these forms:

El domingo **hubo** un accidente muy importante en mi ciudad.
On Sunday **there was** a very important accident in my city.

Cuando yo vivía allí **había** menos tiendas para comprar ropa.
When I was living there, **there were** less shops to buy clothes.

Van a cambiar el programa en mi empresa porque **ha habido** problemas.
They are going to change the program in my company because **there have been** problems.

En Julio no **habría** tanta lluvia aquí.
In July **there wouldn't be** as much rain here (tanto / tanta /tantos / tantas = as much / as many).

Ultimamente **está habiendo** muchas películas sobre historia.
Lately **there "are being"** a lot of movies about History.

Si llegamos tarde **va a haber** que dar explicaciones.
If we arrive late, "**there is going to be**" explaining to do (literally: explanations to give).

Hoy **va a haber** una reunión bastante esperada.
Today **there is going to be** quite an awaited meeting.

A lo largo de la historia **ha habido** muchos barcos.
Throughout history **there have been** many ships (a lo largo de = along / throughout).

¿No **hay** taxis? ¡**Habría** que arreglar esto!
Are there no taxis? "**There should be**" a need to fix this

¡**Hay que** encontrar una solución!
There is the need to find a solution!

Habría que llamar a un técnico para arreglar esto.
We should (there should be an action to) call a technician to fix this

As we can observe in the last sentence, the translation of one of these impersonal constructions can also de "we need to..." or "one should...", but it will depend on the context. Who should call a technician in the last sentence? You? Me? All of us? There is the need to call him, so he should be called... There should be a call to the technician, be it by you, by me, by her... Someone should do it. The translation of this type of sentences in a non-literal way would be something like this:

Hay que tener cuidado con estas cosas = One must be careful with these things
Habrá que esperar para ver qué pasa = We will have to wait to see what happens
No **habría** posibilidad de cambiar = There would not be a possibility to change
Mañana no **habrá** taxis = Tomorrow there will not be taxis (any taxis)
Ha habido muchas películas buenas = There have been many good movies
Habría que estudiar mas = We should study more

IMPERATIVO

The imperative is that tense that allow us to give orders or instructions. We will only be learning the affirmative one (do it! sit down! wait here!) because the negative (don't do it! don't sit down! don't wait here!) is formed in a different way and belongs to the medium level of Spanish. Keep in mind that after knowing the imperative you have seen all the tenses required for the basic level, so you are closer to an average level than to when you started this book. Remember? Aaaah... memories... It's as good moment as any other to let you know how well you've done. You have seen more than 10 different tenses in Spanish mixed with all the other material. After this tense you will be at the threshold of the medium level of Spanish. Keep up the good work! :)

The pronouns in these imperative forms are even more seldom used than with others, so use only the verb but never the pronoun.

Verbs ending in -AR such as NADAR

(Tú) ¡Nada! = Swim! (you)
(Usted) ¡Nade! = Swim! (you sir / madam)
(Nosotros) ¡Nademos! = Let's swim!
(Vosotros) ¡Nadad! = Swim! (you people)
(Ustedes) ¡Naden! = Swim! (you ladies / gentlemen)

Verbs ending in -ER such as COMER

(Tú) ¡Come! = Eat! (you)
(Usted) ¡Coma! = Eat! (you sir / madam)
(Nosotros) ¡Comamos! = Let's eat!
(Vosotros) ¡Comed! = Eat! (you people)
(Ustedes) ¡Coman! = Eat! (you ladies / gentlemen)

Verbs ending in -IR such as VIVIR

(Tú) ¡Vive! = Live! (you)
(Usted) ¡Viva! = Live! (you sir / madam)
(Nosotros) ¡Vivamos! = Let's live!
(Vosotros) ¡Vivid! = Live! (you people)
(Ustedes) ¡Vivan! = Live! (you ladies / gentlemen)

¡**Estudia** más para tu examen! = Study more for your exam!
¡**Vive** y **deja** vivir! = Live and let live (dejar = to let / to allow / to leave something)
¡**Pase**! ¡**Pase**! Está en su casa = Pass! (come in) Pass!, you are at home (pasar = to pass) (this sentence is for you sir/madam so the possessive **SU** must be there instead of **TU**.
¡**Esperemos** el bus aquí! = Let's wait the bus here!
¡**Hablad** más bajo! = Speak lower!
¡**Vean** lo que ha pasado! = See what has happened! (you ladies / gentlemen)
¡**Tened** cuidado con esa puerta! = Be careful with that door (have care / take care with...)

If you check again the forms for verbs ending in **-ER** and in **-IR** you will see that only one letter changes from both groups of endings (com**e**d / viv**i**d), so if you remember that detail differs, you will only need to remember endings for **-AR** and another set for **-ER / -IR**. Those endings in **-D** for "vosotros" are very important because a lot of natives with higher education still make the mistake of pronouncing (or writing) an **R** instead of a **D**. It's a clear mistake, but in informal contexts it might be acceptable to not sound too academic and correct all the time. For regular uses, remember the **-D**.

The exclamation marks ¡! are not an intrinsic part of this tense, they have been added as a resource to differentiate this tense from similar ones. You can give orders or instructions without writing or using those signs. The pronouns that are not there (yo, él, ella...) don't appear because of the impossibility of giving an order to myself or to him / her / them without communicating it directly, thus making it you / you people / you ladies-gentlemen.

As you probably remember, with some tenses it's possible to add the direct object particles at the end:

LLAM**AR** = to call / LLAM**ARTE** = to call you (the Infinitive, normal verb with **TO**)
LLAM**ANDO** = calling / LLAM**ÁNDOTE** = calling you (the gerund, ending in **-ING**)

The third tense that has the direct and indirect object pronouns at the end is precisely the Imperative:

¡LLAM**A**! = call! (you, singular)/ ¡LLÁM**A**ME! = Call me!
¡COMPR**AD**! = buy! (you people) / ¡COMPR**AD**LO! = Buy it!
¡COMPR**ÁD**MELO! = Buy it to me
LLEV**AR** = to take / ¡LLEV**ÁD**SELO! = take it to him / her / them.
¡PREGÚNT**AD**MELO! = ask it to me! (you people ask it to me!)

VOCABULARY: THE ANIMALS / LOS ANIMALES

Mascota = Pet
Bicho = Derogatory term for "animal". Like "bug" instead of "insect" but for all animals.
Perro = Dog
Gato = Cat
Vaca = Cow

Pez = Fish (peces for the plural)

Cerdo = Pig

Oveja = Sheep

Cabra = Goat

Mosca = Fly

Mariposa = Butterfly

Abeja = Bee

Avispa = Wasp

Gusano = Worm

Lobo = Wolf

Oso = Bear

Caballo = Horse

Toro = Bull

Gallina = Hen

Pájaro = Bird

Mascota is for feminine and masculine animals, so: "un perro es una mascota". Bicho has a feminine form, but for one reason or another it always gets used in masculine (bicho / bichos), so even abeja, avispa or mosca get called "bicho" or "bichos" despite being feminine nouns.

Montar a caballo = to ride a horse / horse riding. It's also the verb for bicycles: Montar **EN** bici = to ride a bicycle / to go cycling. As you see, there is a change in the prepositions from one case to the other. **Picar** = to sting (me ha picado una avispa = a wasp has stung me)

Consider that usually for the animals, unless a specific female form exists we will use the common term (considered neutral for animals) and add the words:
"**macho**" = male / "**hembra**" = female

Hay una mosca macho y una mosca hembra en esta foto
There's a male fly and a female fly in this picture

Un pez macho necesita más espacio que un pez hembra
A male fish needs more space than a female fish

Text about animals:

Me gustan mucho los animales. En el sitio en el que vivo hay muchos pájaros distintos y puedes verlos en diferentes parques. No puedo tener un perro porque vivo en un piso, pero tengo peces de colores en un acuario muy grande.

I like animals a lot. In the place where (in which) I live there are many different birds and you can see them in different parks. I can't have a big dog because I live in a flat, but I have fish ("fishes") in a very big aquarium.

Cuando viene algún amigo a casa siempre me pregunta por qué no tengo un gato o algo más común como mascota. Yo siempre respondo que prefiero ver los animales en la naturaleza... en su sitio.

When some friend comes home, he always asks me why I don't have a cat or something more common as a pet. I always answer that I prefer the animals in nature... in their place.

Cuidar de un perro es una gran responsabilidad. Además de la comida y el veterinario hay otros gastos cada mes, también hay que llevarlos a pasear y no puedes dejarlos solos en casa durante demasiado tiempo. Viviendo en una ciudad es difícil poder tener una mascota grande, así que yo prefiero animales más pequeños o esperar y tener una casa en el campo, porque un animal <u>da problemas</u>.

To take care of a dog is a big responsibility. Besides the food and the vet, there are other expenses each month. You also have to (there is the need to) take them for a walk and you can't leave them alone at home for too much time. Living in a city it's difficult to be able to have a big pet, so I prefer smaller animals or to wait and have a house in the forest (fields / countryside) because an animal <u>gives problems</u>.

Dar = To give (yo **doy**, tú **das**, él **da**, etc. The only irregular one is the first one, **doy** as **estoy** from the verb **ESTAR**, so even irregularities are related)
-Da igual = It's the same ("it gives the same result")
-Da problemas = It gives problems

THE GRAPHIC ACCENTS

As you remember, some words in Spanish have a graphic accent that is written from a point on top of the letter to a diagonal on the right side: **á, é, í, ó, ú.** Only the vowels receive a graphic accent on top. The graphic accent indicates that **THE STRESS** of the word is on that syllable, in cases where it could be mistaken, or when two words are written in the same way and we need to differentiate them.

All the words have stress in one syllable or another, but not all the words need a graphic accent. To know where to write them, we need to separate words in 3 groups according to where they have the stress while being pronounced. **WE COUNT SYLLABLES BY THE END** of the word, so keep that in mind. The names of the classes are weird and useless, so just keep in mind where the stress goes. (Palabras = words).

-AGUDAS: Words that have the stress (the strength of the voice) in the last syllable of the word or the first syllable by the end.

__ __ __ @@

-LLANAS: Words that have the stress in the second syllable by the end.

__ __ @@ __

-ESDRÚJULAS: Words that have the stress in the third syllable by the end.

__ @@ __ __

The rules to put a graphic accent are now very easy:

1. We put a graphic accent on the words **AGUDAS** whose **last letter is** an A, E, I, O, U, N, S.

ca-mi-ón: Has the stress in the 1st syllable by the end, finishes in N = ACCENT

cam-pe-ón: Has the stress in the 1st syllable by the end, finishes in N = ACCENT

lla-ma-ré: Has the stress in the 1st syllable by the end, finishes in E = ACCENT

lle - ga -rá: Has the stress in the 1st syllable by the end, finishes in A = ACCENT

re-ga-lar: Has the stress in the 1st syllable by the end, finishes in R = NO ACCENT (because R is not in the group of A,E,I,O,U,N,S)

(camión = truck / campeón = champion / llamaré = I will call / llegará = he-she-it will arrive / regalar = to give as present, to gift)

2. We put a graphic accent on the words **LLANAS** whose **last letter is anything other than** A, E, I, O, U, N, S.

ár-bol: Has the stress in the 2nd syllable by the end, doesn't finish in a,e,i,o,u,n,s = ACCENT
a-zú-car: Has the stress in the 2nd syllable by the end, doesn't finish in a,e,i,o,u,n,s = ACCENT
di-fí-cil: Has the stress in the 2nd syllable by the end, doesn't finish in a,e,i,o,u,n,s = ACCENT

(árbol = tree / azúcar = sugar / difícil = difficult)

3. We put a graphic accent on **ALL THE WORDS** that are **ESDRÚJULAS**. All of them.

o-xí-ge-no = oxygen
a-ca-dé-mi-co = academic
mi-cró-fo-no = microphone

As we mentioned before, some words have an accent to differentiate them from others, especially when they have only one syllable:

Tú = you / Tu = your
Él = he / El = the
Sí = yes / Si = if
Sé = I know / Se = (se hace, se juega = it is done, it is played)

Those are all the examples you need at this level. There are accents that cut syllables made by too many vowels, but those examples are few and too advanced for now, as well as ignored by many native speakers whenever they write, so for now focus on those examples and whenever you see a word with a graphic accent try to see which rule is making it have that accent.

The only accents that are important to remember are the ones of the words ending in **-ÓN**, because those words are almost always agudas and they end in **N**, so they will most of the times require an accent:

Cami**ón** = truck / coraz**ón** = heart / canci**ón** = song / Ram**ón** = Ramon

INSULTS AND SEXUAL TOPICS

It would be hard to understand most movies, shows, or informal conversations, or be proficient in less academic settings if we are unable to use or at least recognize basic swearing or sexual hints. Most countries have their own insults and they sound funny to others, or devoid of toughness, so we should stick with the general international ones.

Puta = Whore (As in, a promiscuous woman or an evil one) **Puto** is also used, but as AN ADJECTIVE, not a noun (un puto, dos putos, tres putos = wrong) for example: ¡Puto español! = Fucking Spaniard!

Zorra = Bitch (Also used in other contexts like "I won this game 6 times! You are my bitch!")

Cabrón = Bastard (but also in a complimentary way, as in "he got promoted without doing anything! ¡Qué cabrón! He is so clever!)

Mierda = Shit (the construction "… de mierda" is an equivalent to "fucking ….." as in "zorra **de mierda**" = fucking bitch

Me cago en... = Literally means "I shit on..." as in the phrase: "¡me cago en todo! = I shit on everything!"

Hijo de puta = Son of a bitch (also complimentary in some contexts, but more risky to get it right, so wait until you really understand where to drop it)

Mariconada = Bullshit (the word "maricón" means faggot, but it's not very used these days. Mariconada is used for unnecessary things, or sissy elements. "I bought myself a pink hat with 2 feathers" "¡Oh! ¡Qué mariconada más grande")

Cojones = Balls (most of the things that in American English mention the ass, in Spanish we mention the balls, usually in the form of " ----- de los cojones" = ¡tráfico de los cojones! = fucking traffic! / fucking ass traffic! "¿Qué cojones haces? = What the fuck are you doing?)

Joder = Fuck! (As an expression alone, just like in English, but also "joder a alguien" = to fuck someone over, to do something bad to a person. "¡No jodas!" = ¡Wow, Fuck!" to express surprise towards some news)

Follar = To Fuck (as a sexual action. "Me gusta follar todos los días = I like to fuck every day"

Mamada = Blowjob (however "comer el rabo or comer la polla" are a bit harsher, and yes, rabo = cock / polla = dick. ¡Qué rabo! / ¡Qué Polla! = What a luck!)

Subnormal / Retrasado = Retard / Retarded. Just as in English, these two insults might be more offensive towards intellectually challenged people than to the person we address, so if they ever invite you to a Spanish-speaking TV don't use them)

Huevos = Balls, but less harsh than cojones. (tocar = to touch, tocahuevos / tocacojones = a person who bothers, a drag, someone who touches your balls and therefore annoys)

Tetas = Breasts (Tits, nothing more to it)

A combination of insults is possible, as long as you don't repeat them (no "fucking fucks" in Spanish) so a good example would be:

¡Me cago en la zorra de los cojones! ¡Joder, hay que ser hija de puta!

I shit on the fuking bitch! Fuck! You really need to be a son of a bitch

(Daughter of a bitch in this case) that "hay que" is translated as: "you really have to..." in this particular case, as explaining that one should really reach those levels of being that evil to do what she hipothetically did in this example of foulmouthery.

As a side note, keep in mind that using the ending **-ito / -ita, or -illo / -illa**, that makes things smaller in Spanish, also has a funny effect with insults, so calling somebody "hijoputilla" or "putita" will be less harsh than calling them the word without making it smaller. Just like the difference in English between: "you are a bitch / you are a little bitch". It can also be extra diminishing if we address them to a man.

Keep in mind that as in many other aspects of life, the gender of the speaker determines the type and amount of curse words we can include in a conversation. Too little will make us disconnected from the rest of the speakers, or will not allow us to convey our true emotions, thus making the communication process less accurate, but too many will make us appear without manners or class. The limit is a bit lower for women than for men, just like in English.

THE CONCEPT OF CULTURAL IMMERSION

We should keep in mind that in a way, a language is a vehicle of culture. By culture we understand the multiple manifestations of a certain group of people, and their contributions to a particular civilization. What I'm getting at is the fact that culture is an important part of anyone's language learning process. It's very hard to understand a language if we choose to ignore key cultural aspects of the places speaking it.

It might seem like an obvious statement, but my point is that if we go back in time to World War II and we are told we have been selected to spy behind enemy lines in Nazi Germany, we would very much hope that the guys, books, and materials teaching us can make us be a part of that culture and that society, or we would otherwise be shot after the first encounters with locals. What was a matter of life and death in past times has become something more optional these days. But we can clearly see how communication will be improved if we understand which facial expressions are appropriate, which subjects to avoid, what type of reactions are perceived positively or negatively, etc. Knowing a language at an advanced level while being unable to participate fully in the culture of its speakers will make most of our communicative possibilities and objectives less efficient.

Also, try to keep in mind that cultural manifestations might originate in an area, but they are not the exclusive property of that area. Yes, the best sushi might be in Japan, but we can also open sushi restaurants in other parts of the world, or cook it at home and do it quite well. The example doesn't have hidden meanings, it just points out that watching Spanish films, checking the Spanish news and having the Spanish radio on your phone is the same, culturally speaking, as eating Japanese food, enjoying Italian operas, or spending our holidays in the Seychelles instead of being culturally limited to our geographical area. Also, do keep in mind that since culture is not a property, but a shared phenomenon once it originates, most of the inventions, ideas and things we have today are far from the place we live in, and that's fine. A new language is just an addition to those other things that makes us who we are.

The type of cultural manifestations we must learn are those valid for the period of time we are interested in (usually the present). A historian interested in Spanish will have to learn more about the cultural things that defined the period he studies, but that is probably not the case of a general speaker, which take us to our next point: The culture you learn must be updated. Are things being done these days as I think? Is the cultural information I already have valid? Do I need to revisit some of the core concepts I once believed in? Am I being presented with a wishful version of reality rather than with an accurate depiction of the facts?

Those misconceptions could negatively influence our interactions in another language. On the one hand we could be seen as mockingly bashing defining parts of someone's culture, and on the other hand we could be seen as outdated, oversimplifying things that are no longer there. In both cases we might be getting a worse reaction than if we take some moments to know about the places whose language we intend to learn.

Without having redefine the concept of "culture", we could be more or less safe if we check the most popular songs in a country the year we plan to visit it, best-selling books, a summary of the political and social situation of the past 5 years, key personalities and what they are famous for, watched shows, food tendencies, common trends, and traditions upheld as well as outdated. In summary, and coming back to the initial simile of this section, we should know about everything that allows us to perfectly merge in, like a WWII spy, should we choose to do so at any given time and for whatever reasons. Even if we never intend to be like a native, having the ability to become exactly like one whenever we please is a very positive point for any language speaker.

SPELLING IN SPANISH / DELETREAR EN ESPAÑOL

At this point, you might want to start talking and having simple tasks. One of the most basic ones is calling to a place and having to give our names, surnames, and the name of the company in which we work, in order for the shipments to arrive correctly, or to register ourselves for some service or in some institution. These is how the letters of the alphabet are called in Spanish:

A = a	**O** = o
B = be	**P** = pe
C = ce	**Q** = cu
D = de	**R** = erre
E = e	**S** = ese
F = efe	**T** = te
G = ge	**U** = u
H = hache	**V** = uve
I = i	**W** = uve doble
J = jota	**X** = equis
K = ka	**Y** = i griega
L = ele	**Z** = ceta
M = eme	
N = ene	
Ñ = eñe	

Be careful not to call the letter W "doble U" or something like that, because that would actually cause the person writing down the word to write U U. This letter is a V and this letter W are two Vs put together. The letter LL is called an "elle" (remember: /ejie/ when pronouncing it) but they took it away from the alphabet for considering it a combination of two Ls and not a letter itself. The most important letter of the list is X = equis, because most forms are filled in by either a tick (tick = marca) or an X (una equis). Spelling your name and address would be like this:

-¿Puedes deletrearme tu nombre? ¿Cómo se escribe?

ANTHONY: **a -ene - te -hache - o - ene - y griega**
JOHNSON: **jota - o - hache -ene - ese - o -ene**
¿Y el nombre de la calle?
GREENFIELD: **ge - erre - e - e - ene - efe - i - e - ele - de**
AVENUE: a - uve - e - ene - u -e

Para temas de ortografía, se usa mucho el verbo "llevar = to take / carry", so people will be asking something like: ¿Ese nombre **lleva** hache? = Does that name have an H?

Pay attention to words you know in other languages, especially in your native one. In Spanish we usually diminish the level of pronunciation to not sound too cocky or appear like a show-off whenever we are talking to other people. This habit is not present in all the Spanish-speaking countries, but it is always to stay somewhere in the middle to not cause rejection whenever we are giving a speech or a presentation.

PRACTICAL TEXTS

Has aprendido mucho. Ahora puedes leer textos en español y no serán muy difíciles. Vamos a hablar de varios temas.
You have learned a lot. Now you can read texts in Spanish and they won't be very difficult. We are going to speak about several subjects (themes).

Presentación / Introducing yourself
Hola, me llamo Antonio, soy de Madrid pero ahora estoy viviendo en León porque trabajo para una empresa internacional. Me gusta nadar, correr los sábados por la tarde y jugar al fútbol con mis amigos cuando tengo tiempo. No veo mucho la tele porque prefiero ver series y programas en mi ordenador. En el futuro me gustaría trabajar en otro país y conocer nuevas culturas.
Hi, my name is Antonio, I am from Madrid but right now I am living in León because I work for

an international company. I like to swim, to run on Saturdays in the afternoons and to play football (international one) with my friends when I have time. I don't watch TV a lot because I prefer to watch series and shows in my computer. In the future I would like to work in another country and to know new cultures.

Viajes / Trips

La última vez que viajé a algún sitio fue a Chile. La gente es muy agradable en ese país y tienen una comida muy rica. Viajé por toda la costa y mientras visitaba esos sitios comí muy bien. El año que viene iré a otros países, y me gustaría poder hablar español con la gente local porque no hablan inglés y es complicado tener conversaciones. Cuando viajo llevo siempre la misma bolsa roja y así es fácil verla desde lejos. Nunca la he perdido.

The last time I traveled to some place it was to Chile. The people are very nice in that country and they have very tasty food. I traveled "by all" the coast and while I was visiting those places I ate very well. The next year (the year that comes) I will go to other countries and I would like to be able ("to can") to speak Spanish with the local people because they don't speak English and it's complicated to have conversations. When I travel I take (carry) always the same red bag, and like that it's easy to see it from afar (from far away). I have never lost it.

Trabajo / Work

Ahora mismo estoy trabajando en una compañía de importación y exportación. Hacemos negocios con muchos países en los que se habla español. Antes trabajaba en otro sitio, pero no me gustaba mi jefe y decidí irme. ¿Por qué trabajar en un sitio donde uno no está bien? Cuando pude cambiar de trabajo fui a la entrevista y después de algunas preguntas me ofrecieron este trabajo. Algunas de las cosas que tengo que hacer ahora son: recibir llamadas de clientes, ir a reuniones, conseguir contratos nuevos y diseñar un plan de marketing para mi departamento.

Right now I am working in an export and import company. We do business with many countries in which Spanish is spoken. Before I was working in another place but I didn't like my boss and I decided to go (ir = to go / irse = to go oneself, to go away). Why working at a place where one is not well? When I was able to change job (change of job) I went to the interview and after some questions I was offered this job. Some of the things that I have to do now are: to receive calls from clients, to go to meetings, to get new contracts and to design a marketing plan for my department.

Aficiones / Hobbies

Me gustan muchas cosas, en especial los deportes al aire libre y los videojuegos. Cuando hace buen tiempo siempre voy al campo y saco fotos de la naturaleza. A veces voy con algunos amigos y hacemos un picnic sobre la hierba. Cuando juego a videojuegos prefiero aquellos en los que puedo diseñar mi propio personaje y puedo cambiar cosas de la aventura. También me gustan los juegos de estrategia y creo que son perfectos para mejorar la inteligencia y aprender cosas nuevas.

I like a lot of things, especially the open-air sports and the video games. When there's a good weather I always go to the countryside and I take pictures (get, take out pictures) of nature. Sometimes I go with some friends and we make a picnic over the grass. When I play video games I prefer those in which I can design my own character and I can change things of the adventure. I also like strategy games and I think they are perfect to improve the intelligence and to learn new things.

Estudios / Studies

Estudié varias cosas cuando estaba en la universidad. Me gradué en historia y empecé un master en ingeniería eléctrica pero era muy difícil y elegí cambiarme a derecho. Hoy en día soy abogado y tengo que seguir estudiando porque siempre hay nuevas leyes, nuevas cosas que aprender, etc. También estoy estudiando algunos idiomas y espero poder especializarme en derecho internacional en el futuro. En la universidad era buen estudiante y siempre preparaba todas las asignaturas.

I studied several things when I was in the university. I graduated in History and I started a Masters in Electrical Engineering but it was very difficult and I chose to change to Law. Nowadays I am a lawyer and I have to go on studying because there are always new laws, new things to learn, etc. I am also studying some languages and I hope (expect) to specialize in International Law in the future. In the university I was a good student and I always prepared all the subjects.

Amigos / Friends

No hay mucha gente con talento para hacer amigos de verdad. Es difícil conocer personas con las que hacer cosas juntos y tener conversaciones interesantes. Por eso, los amigos de verdad son difíciles de encontrar y es bueno cuidarlos y también intentar no tener problemas. Cuando aparece un problema o una discusión, lo mejor es hablar las cosas y explicar los motivos que nos han hecho decir lo que hemos dicho o actuar de una cierta

manera. Con un poco de interés no habrá problemas con los amigos de verdad.

There aren't many people with talent to make real friends. It's difficult to know people with whom to do things together and have interesting conversations. That's why (for that), true friends are difficult to find and we must take care of them and also try not to have problems. When a problem or a discussion appears, the best is to speak the matters (the things) and to explain the motives (reasons) that have made us say what we have said or act in a certain way (manera = way, manner). With a bit of interest there will be no problems with real friends (true friends).

El tiempo / The weather

En esta ciudad siempre está lloviendo. Aunque no sé qué es peor porque en otros sitios tienen nieve y hace mucho más frío. A mí me gustan las ciudades con sol, pero no demasiado. Si hace mucho calor se hace difícil estar en la playa o pasear por la calle, así que es mejor tener un poco de todo para no aburrirse o cansarse de demasiado frío o demasiado calor. Las estaciones son buenas para no vivir siempre en la misma rutina.

In this city it's always raining. Although I don't know what's worse because in other places they have snow and it's much colder (it makes "a lot more of cold"). I like cities with sun, but not too much. If it's too hot, it's (it becomes) difficult to be on the beach or to walk by the street, so it is better to have a bit of everything to not get bored or get tired of too much cold or too much heat. The seasons are good to not live all the time in the same routine.

El futuro / The future

Yo creo que en el futuro tendremos coches autónomos que también podrán volar. Controlar el tráfico en tres dimensiones será más complicado, pero las posibilidades de viajar sin prestar atención a la carretera nos permitirán hacer más cosas. Un viaje de 4 horas en coche se convertirá en una experiencia agradable, ya que podremos ver películas, dormir, escuchar música y muchas cosas más, en lugar de estar centrados en el camino. También creo que en el futuro habrá muchos inventos nuevos, pero me preocupa que con demasiados robots en el mercado de trabajo, habrá mucha gente desempleada.

I think that in the future we will have autonomous cars that will also be able to fly. To control the traffic in 3 dimensions will be more complicated, but the possibilities of travelling without paying attention (prestar = to lend, prestar atención = "to lend attention", to pay attention) to the road will allow us to do more things. A 4-hour trip by car will become (convertirse = become, although the use is more limited than in English) a pleasant experience, since (ya que

= since...) we will be able to watch movies, to sleep, to listen to music and many more things, instead of (en lugar de = instead of) being centered on the way (camino = way). I also believe that in the future there will be many new inventions, but it worries me (preocuparse = to worry oneself) that with too many robots in the job market, there will be many unemployed people (desempleo = unemployment)

Long text with translation at the end

Try to understand the text and then check the translation to help you understand the unknown words. If you write any word on your notebook, remember to do so with some sort of context.

Mis logros en la vida

La mayoría de mis logros en la vida están relacionados con los estudios, los deportes y las relaciones sociales. Intento ser una buena persona, siempre que puedo solucionar un problema con un amigo o con un familiar creo que es un logro pequeño que me ayuda a llegar a grandes cosas para ser una buena persona en la vida.

En estudios mis mayores logros tienen que ver con las cosas en las que me he graduado en el pasado, pero también con las muchas cosas que aprendí mientras estudiaba. Cada desafío académico que una persona se supera le trae a él o a ella un poco más de sabiduría, por lo que es un gran logro por sí mismo. Graduarse de alguna escuela siempre es importante, pero obtener habilidades es lo más importante de todo.

En el deporte conseguí algunos diplomas y medallas en el pasado, pero el mayor logro para mí es mantenerse sano y hacer todas las cosas que me puedan hacer feliz. Creo que cada vez que intentamos algo nuevo mejoramos un poco más en la vida, así que en lugar de centrarse en aquello que puede medirse como logros por otros, me gusta considerar aquellas cosas que me hacen quien soy hoy y todas esas cosas que he aprendido. Por otro lado, sé que todavía soy demasiado joven y que mis logros más importantes están aún por llegar. El futuro siempre trae sorpresas y los logros del pasado son sólo para prepararnos para los retos del futuro. Espero poder superar mis futuros retos y convertirlos en logros.

Translation: My achievements in life

Most of my achievements in life are related with studies, sports and social relations. I try to be a good person, so whenever I can solve a problem with a friend or with a relative I think it's a small achievement that helps me reach bigger things like being a good person in life.

In studies my biggest achievements have to do with the things I have graduated or passed, but also with the many things I have learned while studying. Every academic challenge that a person overcomes brings him or her a bit closer to wisdom, so that's a huge achievement by itself. Graduating some school is always important, but the skills we get there are the most important thing of all.

In sports I got some diplomas and medals in the past, but the biggest achievement for me is to keep healthy and do all the things that can make me happy. I think that every time we try something new we improve a little more in life, so instead of focusing on those things that can be measured as achievements by others, I like to consider those things that make me the person I am today and all those things that I have learned. On the other hand, I know that I am still too young and that my biggest achievements are still to come. The future always brings surprises and the achievements of the past are only there to prepare us for the challenges of the future. I hope I can overcome all my future challenges and turn them into achievements.

REAL TEXT 1

The following is a real article talking about a famous author in Spanish Literature. Your task is to understand everything and look for the words you don't know. If you can work with a text like this, you can be sure your level of Spanish has improved a lot, because we are already dealing with literature, authors, and parts of a biography.

Gabriel José García Márquez nació el 06 de marzo de 1928 en Aracataca, aunque su padre decía que realmente nació en 1927. Creció como un joven tranquilo y tímido, fascinado por lashistorias de su abuelo y las supersticiones de su abuela. Escribiría más tarde García Márquez: "Siento que toda mi escritura ha sido sobre las experiencias del tiempo que pasé con mis abuelos". Su abuelo murió cuando tenía ocho años.

Fue enviado a un internado en Barranquilla. En 1940, cuando tenía doce años, recibió una beca para una escuela secundaria para estudiantes superdotados, dirigidos por jesuitas. A los dieciocho años siguió los deseos de sus padres y se matriculó en la Universidad Nacional de Bogotá como estudiante de derecho en lugar de periodista.

Fue durante este tiempo que García Márquez conoció a su futura mujer. Mientras visitaba a sus padres, conoció a una chica de 13 años con el nombre de Mercedes Barcha Pardo. Después de graduarse en el Liceo Nacional, tomó unas pequeñas vacaciones con sus padres antes de salir para la Universidad. Durante ese tiempo, le propuso matrimonio a su futura mujer. Aunque no estarían casados hasta dentro de catorce años, Mercedes prometió permanecerle fiel.

Como muchos grandes escritores que asisten a la Universidad en carreras que despreciaban, García Márquez encontró que no tenía absolutamente ningún interés en sus estudios, y se convirtió en algo así como un vago. Comenzó a faltar a clases y a descuidar sus estudios. Fue aquí cuando comenzó a escribir de forma seria.

Cien años de soledad fue publicada en junio de 1967 y en una semana todas las copias habían desaparecido. Desde ese momento, el éxito estuvo asegurado, y la novela vendió una nueva edición cada semana, pasando a vender medio millón de copias en el plazo de tres años. Fue traducido a más de dos docenas de idiomas, y ganó cuatro premios internacionales.

En 1981, año en el que fue premiado con la medalla de la Legión de Honor francesa, regresó a Colombia y fue acusado de financiación del M-19, un grupo liberal de guerrilleros. Huyendo de Colombia pidió asilo político en México. En 1982 fue galardonado con el Premio Nobel de literatura y se convirtió en uno de los escritores más importantes en todo el mundo.

REAL TEXT 2

This text is a bit more difficult, and it's part of a university presentation for a lecture about International Studies. This type of text is therefore academic, so if you studied in a Spanish speaking country this is the type of articles you would be presented. You don't need to understand everything on your own, you just have to use the dictionary and realize that if you were to study abroad, you would be able to understand the subjects with the help of a dictionary and a bit of work, which is very good for this stage of your Spanish learning process.

Es importante saber que la educación en Japón está muy condicionada por el final de la Segunda Guerra Mundial, ya que en 1947 se aprueba la Ley Fundamental de Educación que ha seguido utilizándose en mayor o menor medida hasta nuestros días. Una de los puntos más difíciles para los estudiantes japoneses es su alfabeto no-simplificado que se escribe mediante kanjis o símbolos. El problema es que además del alfabeto normal, muchos de los símbolos necesarios para leer un periódico de forma normal no se aprenden hasta la edad de 12 años.

Las guarderías públicas y privadas cuidan y educan a los niños de entre 1 y 5 años. Realizan juegos, actividades al aire libre y aprenden las bases necesarias para socializar más adelante con sus compañeros de colegio. Una curiosidad sobre este sistema es el hecho de que todos los niños llevan el mismo uniforme y la misma cartera ya desde ese ciclo educativo. La idea es conseguir la integración de todos los alumnos en el grupo, que es algo muy importante en la cultura japonesa.

A la educación primaria se entra con 6 o 7 años y es obligatoria. Los alumnos están en este ciclo educativo hasta los 12 años y la mayoría de las instituciones tienen uniformes. En muchas prefecturas japonesas, los deportes y los servicios de comedor son gratuitos, por lo que cualquier alumno tiene facilidades para descubrir las actividades y clubs en los que encaja mejor.

Durante estos años se inculcan valores como la disciplina, el respeto, el compañerismo etc. que están muy presentes en el sistema educativo de ese país. En la educación secundaria inicial los alumnos están desde los 12 hasta los 15 años y también es obligatoria. Sigue el mismo sistema que la educación primaria en cuanto a valores y contenidos, aunque son más avanzados.

La educación secundaria que va desde los 15 hasta los 18 años no es obligatoria por ley, pero a pesar de esto, un 94% de los estudiantes eligen continuar su formación mediante ese ciclo que prepara a los alumnos para la entrada en las universidades de distinto tipo e incluso para las escuelas de formación profesional de nivel avanzado, que en Japón exigen un acceso mediante el sistema educativo común por lo que pueden considerarse más cerca del sistema universitario que de la educación secundaria.

Al graduarse de este ciclo los estudiantes obtienen el acceso a las universidades mediante un examen estatal que mide sus disciplinas y conocimientos y les otorga una puntuación que permite elegir qué universidades y estudios pueden cursar a continuación.

El sistema universitario japonés está fuertemente influido por el sistema de la Commonwealth que se instauró no solo desde la época de la restauración Meiji, sino desde finales de la Segunda Guerra Mundial, por lo que se volvió a refrescar la adhesión a este sistema más o menos internacional. Los alumnos tienen acceso a títulos de grado (B.A, B.Sc), de maestría

(M.A, M. Sc.) y finalmente de doctorado (Ph. D.) como grado final que se suele alcanzar a una edad que se encuentra entre los 27 y los 28 años en caso de que no se hayan sufrido atrasos o adelantos en ninguna de las otras partes

REAL TEXT 3

This one is easier in its subject, but it has a few words that will complement your vocabulary. Why is this easier text the third example? Because this would be the material you have to write in an official Spanish exam, so it's not only about understanding it, it's about considering if you could write something similar without too many mistakes.

Mi casa está en un bosque, pero cerca de la ciudad. Está hecha de madera y tiene un techo rojo, una gran puerta y grandes ventanas para tener más luz. No es muy grande porque entonces sería difícil de limpiar, pero no es demasiado pequeña, por lo que puedo tener amigos de visita a menudo.

La madera es ligera y resistente, es un poco gruesa así que puede proteger contra la nieve y las lluvias. Las ventanas tienen doble vidrio por la misma razón y también para evitar ruidos de fuera cuando estoy durmiendo. Me gustaría pintarla de algún color bonito, pero el techo debe ser de color rojo y tener bastante lugar para una chimenea. La chimenea es de ladrillo, y va muy bien con el diseño de la casa.

Hay un camino para llegar a la casa con un montón de lámparas solares. Ayudan a saber dónde uno está caminando cuando está oscuro. Alrededor de la casa hay un jardín con flores y plantas. Es muy bonito, tendrá especias, así como diversas flores y plantas porque la jardinería es un buen pasatiempo y puede ayudar a ahorrar algo de dinero también. Me gustaría tener tulipanes de diferentes colores.

También hay una sauna en un cuarto con una ventana que permite ver lo que está sucediendo fuera de la vivienda, pero la gente no puede ver el interior. Hay mucho espacio dentro, tal vez para una o dos personas. Los árboles cercanos tendrán flores en verano, siempre he pensado que los cerezos huelen muy bien.

La casa tiene una verja metálica alrededor con varias medidas de seguridad y una puerta de que se puede abrir desde el coche. El garaje tiene espacio para dos coches y un par de bicicletas, así como herramientas y un armario de almacenamiento para materiales y cosas de jardinería. La biblioteca puede verse desde el exterior, con muchos libros dentro, porque me gusta leer, y habrá cortinas en el resto de las ventanas que impedirían a los vecinos ver lo que está sucediendo.

Para alguien viendo la casa desde el exterior parecerá natural y elegante. Una casa que se mezcla bien con el medio ambiente. Finalmente, la ubicación será dentro de un bosque, pero cerca de la ciudad así puedo ir en bicicleta por si quiero comprar algo. En invierno la casa parecerá como de un cuento de hadas, en verano parece un buen lugar para descansar y una mesa con algunas sillas se pueden poner fuera para pasar una tarde agradable con algo de beber y de comer.

TECHNIQUES AND HINTS TO IMPROVE YOUR SPANISH SKILLS

-Keep a small notebook with you. No, I'm not kidding... they still sell them. By small I mean "able to fit a pocket". I am perfectly aware that electronic devices can take notes and all that. It's not the same. Apparently the results of handwritten notes whenever we find a word we want to remember or something to check later, are more promising than digital notes.

-Know your language. Imagine if somebody said: "La la laaaa... I am going to India to learn English because English is an official language in that country and it's probably the same learning there than in Oxford or Harvard... it's all English, right?" Of course you couldn't actually explain them that even though India was a British colony for decades and decades, and English is indeed an official national language there, the results won't be the same as learning in Princeton or Cambridge. Spanish is exactly the same.

It's not very nice to say it openly, but if you wish to listen to the radio, the TV, movies, shows, or travel to a Spanish-speaking area, during this stage of your learning process let it be to places where normative Spanish is spoken. For me it would be easier to say that all varieties are nice and beautiful, but research shows that normative varieties of a language are the right ones for learners, and if you wish to pick a cool accent from India or from Bolivia, do it after you are an advanced speaker. Learn some of the differences between different Spanish areas, and different Latin American areas to know what to expect.

-Download audio programs of the subjects you like. Videos are of course cool, but audio files allow us to do other things without having to look at a screen all the time. Getting information about literature, video games, history, or whatever our interests are will make it more interesting for us to train our listening skills.

-Movies and shows for children. At this stage it would be awesome to watch a movie and understand 60 or 70% of everything they say, right? Well, the best way is to watch animation movies for children. Disney's classics, Kung Fu Panda, etc. The voice actors from Spain have a perfect diction and an outstanding pronunciation. The vocabulary will not be hard because those are movies children should be able to understand. The best way to listen to them is in Spanish with English subtitles at first, and with Spanish subtitles on the second viewing. Write down any terms or words you think are worth remembering.

-Ask for corrections. People from major languages (English, Spanish, French...) have the habit of never correcting the speakers who try to communicate in their languages, thinking that it is not polite to correct people who are making an effort. It's a misconception. As a learner, it is much more necessary to improve than to not have our feelings hurt and end up memorizing mistakes or wrong constructions. Insist a lot on being corrected and explain that it's good for you.

The brain tends to validate mistakes after using them several times without a negative response, in some sort of thing like:
"-This must be right... I have heard it a dozen times!"
"-Yes, you have heard it a dozen times because YOU have said it a dozen times and nobody cared to correct you until now"

-Careful with the dictionaries. No... Really... CAREFUL. They are not a shopping list. You can't just go to look for a word, get the first term that appears and use it right away. You have to find context to that term in search engines and with real examples. A term in a dictionary can be outdated because dictionaries don't get re-written every 3 or 4 years, they just get the old one and add new terms. Is "pardon" a word in the dictionary? YES. Can I use it as a synonym of "forgiveness"? NO, because we are not characters in a Shakespearian story... So, is the word useless and outdated? NO, a presidential pardon would be very weird if it were expressed like "a presidential sorry", so the word is fine where it is and we must get it with the right context and avoid assuming that if a term in English has 3 possible contexts, in Spanish it will have the same ones.

CONCLUSION

If you have finished the book, I must say you did very well. As you can see Spanish is very easy to learn when you have the right method and with a bit more effort you can also feel comfortable in a medium level, and then in an advanced one. In the book for medium level we will be seeing the advanced tenses (If I **had known** you needed my help I **would have gone** there earlier) together with many other terms and verbs we need to develop your skills. We will also be introducing real life situations and scenarios related to social interactions, job interviews, working life, flirting, writing skils, etc.) If the book for medium level hasn't been published yet, you can have a look at a novel I wrote called: "Abcalia: El Viaje de los Sueños" because I designed it precisely for students of Spanish (it won a small award so it can't be too bad, can it?)

Thank you for learning Spanish with me, and see you in the next book:

"A Good Spanish Book! : Medium Level Spanish Course for Intermediate Students"

THE END

TAKE NOTES HERE 1/3

TAKE NOTES HERE 2/3

TAKE NOTES HERE 3/3

Printed in Poland
by Amazon Fulfillment
Poland Sp. z o.o., Wrocław